CAKES & BAKING

Edited by Norma MacMillan and Wendy James
Home economist Gilly Cubitt

ORBIS PUBLISHING London

Introduction

It is always fun to cook something special for tea. We
have selected a wide range of recipes – breads, cakes,
gâteaux, pastries and biscuits – some for everyday and
some for special occasions.

Both imperial and metric measures are given for each recipe;
you should follow only one set of measures as they are not
direct conversions. All spoon measures are level unless
otherwise stated. Pastry quantities are based on the amount
of flour used. Fresh yeast may be substituted for dried
yeast. Where the recipe calls for dried yeast, use twice
the quantity.

Photographs were supplied by Editions Atlas, Editions Atlas/Cedus, Editions Atlas/Masson,
Editions Atlas/Zadora, Cadbury, Gales Honey, Archivio IGDA, Lavinia Press Agency,
Orbis GmbH, Tate and Lyle Refineries Ltd

The material in this book has previously appeared in *The Complete Cook*

First published 1981 in Great Britain by Orbis Publishing Limited,
20–22 Bedfordbury, London WC2

© EDIPEM, Novara 1976
© 1978, 1979, 1980, 1981 Orbis Publishing, London

ISBN 0-85613-376-0
Printed in Singapore

Contents

Wholemeal bread

Overall timing 3 hours minimum

Freezing Suitable

Makes 2–4 loaves

1 tbsp	Brown sugar	15 ml
1½ pints	Lukewarm water	850 ml
1 oz	Dried yeast	25 g
3 lb	Wholemeal flour	1.4 kg
1 tbsp	Salt	15 ml
1 oz	Lard	25 g

Dissolve 1 teasp (5 ml) of the sugar in 9 fl oz (250 ml) of the warm water in a bowl. Sprinkle the dried yeast on top. Leave for about 10 minutes till frothy.

Mix flour, salt and the remaining sugar in a bowl. Rub in the lard, then add the yeast liquid and the rest of the water. Mix to scone-like dough. Knead the dough thoroughly till it feels firm and elastic and no longer sticky. This should take 5–10 minutes. Shape the dough into a ball and place in an oiled polythene bag. Leave to rise till doubled in size.

Turn the dough on to a board and knead again till firm. Divide into two or four and flatten each piece firmly with the knuckles to knock out air. Shape and place in loaf tins.

Brush the tops with a little salted water and put each tin into an oiled polythene bag. Leave to rise till the dough comes to just over the top of the tin and springs back when pressed with a floured finger – about 1 hour at room temperature.

Preheat the oven to 450°F (230°C) Gas 8. Bake the loaves for 30–40 minutes. Turn out to cool on a wire rack.

Caraway seed bread

Overall timing 1½ hours plus proving

Freezing Suitable: refresh in hot oven for 10 minutes

Makes 2 small or 1 large loaf

1 lb	Strong plain flour	450 g
1½ oz	Caster sugar	40 g
2 teasp	Dried yeast	2x5 ml
5 tbsp	Lukewarm water	5x15 ml
4 fl oz	Lukewarm milk	120 ml
1 teasp	Salt	5 ml
2 tbsp	Caraway seeds	2x15 ml
4 oz	Softened butter	125 g
2	Eggs	2
1 tbsp	Milk	15 ml

Mix together 4 oz (125 g) flour, 1 teasp (5 ml) sugar, the yeast, water and milk in a large bowl. Cover and leave in a warm place for about 20 minutes till frothy.

Mix remaining flour with salt, remaining sugar and caraway seeds. Add to yeast mixture with butter and beaten eggs. Mix well to a soft dough. Turn on to a lightly floured surface and knead till smooth and elastic. Cover and leave to rise until doubled in size.

Turn dough on to a lightly floured surface and knead till dough is firm again. Shape into two rolls about 6 inches (15 cm) long. Place on greased and floured baking tray. Make three cuts across top of each loaf. Brush with milk. Cover with polythene bag and leave to rise until loaves double in size.

Preheat the oven to 400°F (200°C) Gas 6. Bake the loaves for 30–35 minutes. Cool on a wire rack.

Quick cottage loaf

Overall timing 1½ hours

Freezing Suitable

Makes 1 loaf

1 oz	Fresh yeast	25 g
12 fl oz	Lukewarm water	350 ml
1 tablet	Vitamin C	25 mg
1¼ lb	Strong plain flour	600 g
2 teasp	Salt	2x5 ml
1 teasp	Sugar	5 ml
½ oz	Lard	15 g

Blend the fresh yeast with the warm water. Crush vitamin tablet and add to the yeast liquid.

Sift the flour, salt and sugar into a bowl and rub in lard. Add the yeast liquid and mix to a dough that leaves the bowl clean. Turn the dough on to a lightly floured surface and knead till smooth and elastic.

To shape dough into a cottage loaf, divide it into two pieces with one about a third bigger than the other. Shape both into rounds and place smaller one on top. Press handle of wooden spoon through centre of both pieces. Place on baking tray and cover with oiled polythene. Leave to rise for 40–50 minutes.

Preheat the oven to 450°F (230°C) Gas 8. Dust loaf with flour and bake for 30–35 minutes.

Soda bread

Overall timing 1 hour

Freezing Suitable: bake after thawing

Makes 1 loaf

1 lb	Strong white or white and wholemeal flour	450 g
1 teasp	Salt	5 ml
2 teasp	Bicarbonate of soda	2x5 ml
4 teasp	Cream of tartar	4x5 ml
1 oz	Fat	25 g
9 fl oz	Milk	250 ml

Preheat the oven to 425°F (220°C) Gas 7.

Sift the flour, salt, soda and cream of tartar into a bowl. Rub in the fat and add enough milk to make a soft dough. Knead for 1 minute, then shape into a ball and place on a greased baking tray. Mark with a cross, cutting almost to the base of the dough.

Bake for 40–50 minutes till well risen, lightly browned and firm underneath.

Milk buns

Overall timing About 3 hours

Freezing Suitable

Makes about 15

2 teasp	Dried yeast	2x5 ml
¼ pint	Lukewarm milk	150 ml
9 oz	Plain flour	250 g
4 teasp	Caster sugar	4x5 ml
½ teasp	Salt	2.5 ml
3½ oz	Butter	100 g

Mix yeast, all but 2 tbsp (2x15 ml) milk, 2 oz (50 g) flour and 3 teasp (3x5 ml) sugar to make a batter. Leave till frothy.

Add rest of flour and salt to batter. Mix by hand to soft dough that leaves bowl clean. Knead till smooth and no longer sticky. Leave to rise for 1 hour in warm place.

Cut butter into small pieces. Make a hollow in dough and drop in a few pieces of butter. Knead or squeeze into dough. Continue adding butter in this way till dough becomes silky and smooth. Divide into egg-size pieces and shape into rolls. Place on greased baking tray. Lightly mark a cross on each. Leave to rise till doubled in size.

Preheat the oven to 375°F (190°C) Gas 5.

Heat remaining milk and sugar and brush over rolls. Bake for 30 minutes till golden brown. Cool on wire rack.

Fruit and nut bread

Overall timing 35 minutes plus rising

Freezing Suitable

Makes 1 loaf

7 fl oz	Lukewarm milk	200 ml
4 teasp	Dried yeast	4x5 ml
2½ oz	Caster sugar	65 g
1 lb	Strong plain flour	450 g
1 teasp	Salt	5 ml
4 oz	Butter	125 g
2 oz	Stoned prunes	50 g
2 oz	Dried figs	50 g
2 oz	Sultanas	50 g
4 oz	Mixed nuts	125 g
1	Egg	1
1 tbsp	Icing sugar	15 ml

Mix ¼ pint (150 ml) milk with yeast and 1 teasp (5 ml) sugar. Leave till frothy.

Sift flour and salt into a large bowl. Add yeast mixture, melted butter, remaining sugar, chopped fruit and nuts and remaining milk. Mix to a soft dough. Leave to rise till doubled in size.

Knead until smooth. Shape into a rectangle and place in 2 lb (900 g) loaf tin. Leave to prove until doubled in size.

Preheat the oven to 425°F (225°C) Gas 7. Brush top of loaf with lightly beaten egg and bake for 15 minutes. Cover top with grease-proof paper and reduce heat to 400°F (200°C) Gas 6. Bake for further 20–30 minutes. Dredge with icing sugar and serve warm.

Sesame bread

Overall timing 2 hours plus proving

Freezing Suitable

Makes 2 loaves

6	Saffron strands	6
¼ pint	Lukewarm milk	150 ml
4 fl oz	Lukewarm water	120 ml
1 tbsp	Dried yeast	15 ml
4 teasp	Caster sugar	4x5 ml
1 lb	Strong plain flour	450 g
2 oz	Butter	50 g
2	Eggs	2
½ teasp	Salt	2.5 ml
2 tbsp	Sesame seeds	2x15 ml

Mix together saffron, all but 2 tbsp (2x15 ml) milk, the water, yeast, 1 teasp (5 ml) sugar and 2 tbsp (2x15 ml) flour. Leave in a warm place till frothy.

Melt butter and cool, then beat into batter with one egg and the remaining milk and sugar. Sift remaining flour and the salt over batter and mix to a soft dough. Knead till smooth. Leave to rise till doubled in size.

Knock back the dough. Knead till smooth and divide into six pieces. Roll into sausages about 9 inches (23 cm) long. Moisten ends of sausages with beaten egg. Plait three together, pinching together at both ends to seal. Repeat with remaining three sausages and arrange on greased baking tray. Leave to rise till doubled in size.

Preheat the oven to 375°F (190°C) Gas 5. Brush plaits carefully with beaten egg, then sprinkle with sesame seeds. Bake for about 35 minutes. Cool on wire rack.

Lemon buns

Overall timing 1 hour plus cooling

Freezing Suitable: refresh in 400°F (200°C) Gas 6 oven for 10 minutes

Makes 12

2 oz	Caster sugar	50 g
5 tbsp	Lukewarm milk	5 x 15 ml
2 teasp	Dried yeast	2 x 5 ml
8 oz	Strong plain flour	225 g
	Salt	
	Grated rind of 2 lemons	
1	Egg	1
1	Egg yolk	1
2 oz	Butter	50 g

Dissolve ½ teasp (2.5 ml) of the sugar in the milk and sprinkle the yeast on top. Leave in a warm place for 15 minutes till frothy.

Sift the flour and a pinch of salt into a bowl and stir in the remaining sugar and lemon rind. Add the yeast mixture, beaten egg and yolk and melted butter and mix to a stiff dough. Divide between greased 12-hole bun tray. Cover with oiled polythene and leave to rise in a warm place till doubled in size.

Preheat the oven to 375°F (190°C) Gas 5. Bake the buns for about 25 minutes till well risen. Cool on a wire rack.

Brioche

Overall timing $1\frac{1}{4}$ hours plus proving

Freezing Suitable: shape dough and bake after thawing

Makes 1 large or 12 small

2 teasp	Caster sugar	2x5 ml
2 tbsp	Lukewarm water	2x15 ml
2 teasp	Dried yeast	2x5 ml
8 oz	Strong plain flour	225 g
	Salt	
2 oz	Butter	50 g
2	Eggs	2
	Milk for glazing	

Dissolve $\frac{1}{2}$ teasp (2.5 ml) sugar in water and sprinkle yeast on top. Leave till frothy.

Sift flour, a pinch of salt and remaining sugar into a large bowl. Add yeast mixture, melted butter and eggs and mix to a soft dough. Knead till smooth and glossy. Leave to rise in a warm place till doubled in size.

Knock back dough and knead for 3–4 minutes till smooth. To make one large brioche, cut off one-quarter of the dough and shape both pieces into balls. Place large one in lightly greased 8 inch (20 cm) brioche tin and push a finger down through centre to base. Place smaller ball in indentation and press down lightly.

To make 12 small brioches, divide dough into 12 pieces and remove one-quarter from each. Shape all pieces into balls. Place each large ball in a 3 inch (7.5 cm) brioche tin, push a finger down through centre, then top with small balls, pressing down lightly. Leave to rise till doubled in size.

Preheat the oven to 450°F (230°C) Gas 8. Brush each brioche with milk and bake for 8–10 minutes (small) or 15–20 minutes (large) till well risen and golden. Serve warm.

Bagels

Overall timing 1¼ hours plus proving and cooling

Freezing Suitable: refresh from frozen in 400°F (200°C) Gas 6 oven for 10 minutes

Makes 10

1 teasp	Caster sugar	5 ml
6 tbsp	Lukewarm water	6x15 ml
1 teasp	Dried yeast	5 ml
9 oz	Strong plain flour	250 g
1 teasp	Salt	5 ml
1	Egg	1
1 tbsp	Oil	15 ml
1	Egg yolk	1
1 teasp	Caraway seeds	5 ml
1 teasp	Poppy seeds	5 ml
1 teasp	Coarse salt	5 ml

Dissolve sugar in water and sprinkle yeast on top. Leave till frothy.

Sift flour and salt into a large bowl. Add egg, oil and yeast mixture. Mix to a soft dough. Knead till smooth and glossy. Leave to rise till doubled in size.

Knock back dough and knead till smooth. Divide into 10 equal portions and roll into sausage shapes about 7 inches (18 cm) long. Wrap sausage shapes round to make rings and pinch ends together to seal. Smooth joins by rocking dough on a floured surface. Arrange on a baking tray, cover with oiled polythene and leave to rise till almost doubled in bulk.

Preheat oven to 425°F (220°C) Gas 7.

Poach bagels, in batches, in boiling water for 2 minutes, turning them once. Remove from the pan with a draining spoon and arrange on a floured baking tray.

When all the bagels are ready, brush them with egg yolk. Sprinkle some with caraway seeds, some with poppy seeds and some with coarse salt. Bake for about 15 minutes till crisp and golden brown. Cool on a wire rack.

Cheese yeast cake

Overall timing 2½ hours

Freezing Suitable: reheat in 350°F (180°C) Gas 4 oven for 15–20 minutes, then add jam and almonds

To serve 16

8 oz	Plain flour	225 g
2 oz	Caster sugar	50 g
3 teasp	Dried yeast	3x5 ml
6 tbsp	Lukewarm milk	6x15 ml
1 oz	Softened butter	25 g
1	Egg	1
	Pinch of salt	
Topping		
2 oz	Butter	50 g
8 oz	Curd cheese	225 g
4 tbsp	Cold custard	4x15 ml
	Grated rind of 1 lemon	
1	Egg	1
4 oz	Caster sugar	125 g
1½ lb	Dessert apples	700 g
4 tbsp	Apricot jam	4x15 ml
2 oz	Flaked almonds	50 g

Mix together 2 oz (50 g) flour, 1 teasp (5 ml) sugar, yeast and milk. Leave till frothy.

Add remaining flour and sugar, the softened butter, egg and salt. Mix well to form a soft dough. Knead till smooth, then leave to rise for 30 minutes in a warm place.

Roll out dough and line bottom of greased 7x11 inch (18x28 cm) roasting tin.

Preheat oven to 400°F (200°C) Gas 6.

To make topping, melt butter and brush half over dough. Beat cheese with custard, lemon rind, egg and sugar. Spread evenly over dough. Peel, core and slice apples. Arrange on top of creamed mixture. Brush with remaining melted butter and bake for 45 minutes.

Remove cake from tin. Heat jam and spread over apples. Sprinkle with almonds and serve warm.

Danish pastries

Overall timing 2 hours including chilling

Freezing Suitable

Makes 15

1½ oz	Caster sugar	40 g
3 fl oz	Lukewarm milk	90 ml
1 teasp	Dried yeast	5 ml
9 oz	Plain flour	250 g
½ teasp	Salt	2.5 ml
6 oz	Butter	175 g
	Almond paste	
1	Egg	1
4 oz	Icing sugar	125 g

Dissolve 1 teasp (5 ml) sugar in milk and sprinkle yeast on top. Leave till frothy. Sift flour and salt into bowl, rub in ½ oz (15 g) butter and add rest of sugar and yeast mixture. Mix to a dough. Shape remaining butter into an oblong. Roll out dough into an oblong twice size of butter. Place butter in centre and wrap dough round.

Turn dough so folds are at sides. Roll into an oblong three times longer than it is wide. Fold bottom third up, top third down. Chill for 10 minutes. Repeat turning, rolling and chilling twice.

Roll out dough into oblong, 15x9 inches (38x23 cm), cut into 15 squares and shape as below:

Cockscombs: Put almond paste in centre of each and fold in half, sealing with beaten egg. Make cuts in folded edge, almost to cut edges; spread out in a fan shape. Envelopes: Put almond paste in centre of each and fold opposite corners to centre, securing tips with beaten egg. Windmills: Make diagonal cuts from each corner almost to centre. Place almond paste in centre and fold one corner of each triangle to it. Press firmly to secure. Arrange shapes on baking trays and prove for 20 minutes.

Preheat the oven to 425°F (220°C) Gas 7. Brush with beaten egg and bake for 18 minutes. Mix icing sugar with 2 tbsp (2x15 ml) water and trickle over hot pastries.

Italian fruit bread

Overall timing 1½ hours plus proving

Freezing Suitable: reheat in 350°F (180°C) Gas 4 oven for 10 minutes

To serve 5

12 oz	Strong plain flour	350 g
4 teasp	Dried yeast	4x5 ml
2 oz	Caster sugar	50 g
¼ pint	Lukewarm milk	150 ml
¼ teasp	Salt	1.25 ml
2 oz	Pine nuts	50 g
2 oz	Candied peel	50 g
2 oz	Seedless raisins	50 g
2 oz	Butter	50 g
1	Egg	1
1 tbsp	Marsala	15 ml

Mix together 4 oz (125 g) flour, the yeast, 1 teasp (5 ml) sugar and the milk to a smooth batter. Leave till frothy.

Sift remaining flour and the salt into a large bowl. Add remaining sugar, the pine nuts, candied peel and raisins. Stir melted butter, beaten egg and Marsala into frothy batter, then add to fruit mixture. Mix to a soft dough. Turn out on to a lightly floured surface and knead till smooth and glossy. Cover with oiled polythene and leave to rise till doubled in size.

Knock back dough and knead till smooth. Shape into a smooth ball and place on greased baking tray. Leave to prove till doubled in size.

Preheat the oven to 400°F (200°C) Gas 6. Score a cross on top of the ball and bake for 10 minutes. Reduce the heat to 350°F (180°C) Gas 4 and bake for a further 25 minutes. Cool on a wire rack.

Spicy fruit bread

Overall timing 1½ hours plus proving

Freezing Suitable: reheat in 350°F (180°C) Gas 4 oven for 20 minutes

To serve 8

3 oz	Light soft brown sugar	75 g
¼ pint	Milk	150 ml
4 teasp	Dried yeast	4x5 ml
12 oz	Strong plain flour	350 g
½ teasp	Salt	2.5 ml
1 teasp	Ground cinnamon	5 ml
	Ground cloves	
3 oz	Softened butter	75 g
1	Egg	1
6 oz	Sultanas	175 g
2 oz	Currants	50 g

Dissolve ½ teasp (2.5 ml) sugar in all but 2 tbsp (2x15 ml) of the milk and sprinkle yeast on top. Leave in warm place till frothy.

Sift the flour, salt, cinnamon and a pinch of cloves into a large bowl. Add the yeast mixture, butter, egg, remaining sugar, the sultanas and currants. Mix to a soft dough. Knead the dough on a floured surface till glossy. Wrap in oiled polythene and leave to rise till doubled in size.

Turn the dough out on to a floured surface and knead till smooth. Shape into a thick sausage and place on a greased baking tray. Cover with oiled polythene and leave to prove till doubled in size.

Preheat the oven to 400°F (200°C) Gas 6. Brush the dough with the reserved milk and bake for about 40 minutes. Cool on a wire rack.

Chelsea buns

Overall timing 1 hour plus proving

Freezing Suitable

Makes 6

1 lb	Strong plain flour	450 g
7 tbsp	Caster sugar	7x15 ml
8 fl oz	Lukewarm milk	225 ml
4 teasp	Dried yeast	4x5 ml
4 oz	Butter	125 g
1	Egg	1
4 oz	Mixed dried fruit	125 g
1 teasp	Mixed spice	5 ml

Mix 4 oz (125 g) flour with 1 teasp (5 ml) sugar, 7 fl oz (200 ml) milk and the yeast to a smooth batter. Leave till frothy.

Sift remaining flour and 4 teasp (4x5 ml) sugar into a bowl and rub in 3 oz (75 g) butter. Add egg and yeast mixture and mix to a soft dough. Knead till smooth and glossy. Leave to rise till doubled in size.

Knock back dough and knead till smooth. Roll out to a 9 inch (23 cm) square. Brush remaining butter, melted, over dough. Mix all but 1 tbsp (15 ml) of remaining sugar with fruit and spice and sprinkle over dough. Roll up, then cut across into six thick slices. Arrange, cut sides up, in greased 9x6 inch (23x15 cm) roasting tin, leaving equal space between. Prove till slices join together.

Preheat oven to 375°F (190°C) Gas 5. Brush buns with remaining milk and sprinkle with remaining sugar. Bake for about 35 minutes till golden. Cool on wire rack.

Pretzels

Overall timing 1 hour plus proving

Freezing Suitable: reheat in 375°F (190°C) Gas 5 oven for 5–10 minutes

Makes about 30

½ teasp	Caster sugar	2.5 ml
7 fl oz	Lukewarm water	200 ml
2 teasp	Dried yeast	2x5 ml
10 oz	Strong plain flour	275 g
1 teasp	Salt	5 ml
1 teasp	Poppy seeds	5 ml
1 oz	Butter	25 g
2	Eggs	2
2 tbsp	Coarse salt	2x15 ml

Dissolve sugar in water and sprinkle yeast on top. Leave in warm place till frothy.

Sift flour and salt into a bowl and stir in poppy seeds, yeast mixture, melted butter and one egg. Mix to soft dough. Leave to rise till doubled in size.

Knead till smooth. Break off small pieces and tie into loose knots, tucking ends in. Arrange pretzels on greased baking trays. Leave to prove till doubled in size.

Preheat the oven to 400°F (200°C) Gas 6. Beat remaining egg and brush over pretzels. Sprinkle with coarse salt and bake for about 10 minutes till crisp and golden. Cool on wire rack.

Currant buns

Overall timing 2¼ hours

Freezing Suitable

Makes 12

1 lb	Strong plain flour	450 g
3 oz	Caster sugar	75 g
1 tbsp	Dried yeast	15 ml
11 fl oz	Lukewarm milk	325 ml
½ teasp	Salt	2.5 ml
1 teasp	Mixed spice	5 ml
4 oz	Currants	125 g
2 oz	Butter	50 g
1	Egg	1

Mix together 2 oz (50 g) flour, 1 teasp (5 ml) sugar, the yeast and ½ pint (300 ml) milk to a batter. Leave till frothy.

Sift remaining flour, salt and spice into a mixing bowl. Add currants, 2 oz (50 g) sugar, the yeast mixture, melted butter and egg. Mix to a soft dough. Knead till smooth and elastic. Leave to rise till doubled in size.

Knock back dough, then divide into 12 pieces. Knead each piece into a smooth bun. Place on baking trays, cover and leave to prove till doubled in size.

Preheat the oven to 375°F (190°C) Gas 5.

To make glaze, dissolve remaining sugar in rest of milk and brush lightly over the buns. Bake for 15–20 minutes. While still hot, brush with remaining glaze.

Jam doughnuts

Overall timing 3–3½ hours including rising

Freezing Suitable: reheat from frozen in 400°F (200°C) Gas 6 oven for 8 minutes

Makes 12

8 oz	Strong plain flour	225 g
2 teasp	Dried yeast	2x5 ml
5 tbsp	Caster sugar	5x15 ml
6 tbsp	Lukewarm milk	6x15 ml
¼ teasp	Salt	1.25 ml
1½ oz	Butter	40 g
1	Egg	1
	Oil for frying	
	Jam	

Mix together 2 oz (50 g) flour, the yeast, 2 teasp (2x5 ml) sugar and the milk to a batter. Leave till frothy.

Sift remaining flour and salt into bowl. Add yeast mixture, melted butter and beaten egg and mix to a soft dough. Knead till smooth and elastic. Leave to rise till doubled in size.

Knock back dough, divide into 12 and shape into balls. Leave to prove.

Heat the oil in a deep-fryer to 360°F (180°C). Press a deep hole in each dough ball and fill with about 1 teasp (5 ml) jam. Seal jam in well by pinching dough together. Deep fry for about 10 minutes. Drain on kitchen paper and roll in remaining sugar while still hot.

Irish tea brack

Overall timing 1¾ hours plus overnight soaking

Freezing Suitable

To serve 12

1 lb	Mixed dried fruit	450 g
¼ pint	Hot black tea	150 ml
2 tbsp	Irish whiskey	2x15 ml
8 oz	Dark soft brown sugar	225 g
8 oz	Self-raising flour	225 g
2 teasp	Mixed spice	2x5 ml
2	Eggs	2

Place dried fruit in a bowl with hot tea and whiskey. Leave to soak overnight.

Next day preheat the oven to 350°F (180°C) Gas 4.

Add the sugar to the soaked fruit, then sift the flour and spice over. Beat in the eggs to give a soft consistency. Spread the mixture in a greased and lined 2 lb (900 g) loaf tin and smooth the top.

Bake for about 1½ hours till firm and springy to the touch (cover cake lightly with grease-proof paper halfway through cooking to prevent top overbrowning). Cool on a wire rack. Cut into thick slices and spread with butter to serve.

Boiled fruit cake

Overall timing 2 hours plus cooling

Freezing Suitable

To serve 16

4 oz	Dried apricots	125 g
4 oz	Dried figs	125 g
8 fl oz	Milk	220 ml
6 oz	Dark soft brown sugar	175 g
2 tbsp	Black treacle	2x15 ml
4 oz	Butter	125 g
4 oz	Seedless raisins	125 g
8 oz	Self-raising flour	225 g
1 tbsp	Mixed spice	15 ml
$\frac{1}{2}$ teasp	Bicarbonate of soda	2.5 ml
2	Eggs	2
1	Orange	1
6 tbsp	Apricot jam	6x15 ml
2 tbsp	Caster sugar	2x15 ml

Mixed glacé fruits and whole nuts

Cut apricots and figs into strips. Put milk, sugar, treacle, butter and fruits in a saucepan and bring to the boil, stirring to dissolve sugar. Boil for 3 minutes, then remove from heat and cool.

Preheat the oven to 325°F (170°C) Gas 3.

Sift flour, spice and soda over boiled mixture and beat in with eggs. Grate rind from orange and add. Mix well. Pour into greased and lined 8 inch (20 cm) square cake tin and smooth top. Bake for $1\frac{1}{4}$–$1\frac{1}{2}$ hours till a skewer inserted in centre comes out clean. Cool on a wire rack.

To make topping, put jam and caster sugar in pan and bring to boil, stirring. Sieve mixture, then brush over top of cake. Arrange glacé fruit and nuts decoratively on top and brush with remaining jam. Leave to cool and set before cutting into slices or squares to serve.

Tunisian fruit and nut cake

Overall timing 1¾ hours

Freezing Suitable

To serve 8

1 oz	Toasted hazelnuts	25 g
2 oz	Toasted pistachios	50 g
1	Orange	1
5	Eggs	5
8 oz	Caster sugar	225 g
4 oz	Dried breadcrumbs	125 g
2 oz	Plain flour	50 g
1 teasp	Baking powder	5 ml
½ teasp	Bicarbonate of soda	2.5 ml
½ teasp	Ground cinnamon	2.5 ml
4 oz	Sultanas	125 g

Preheat the oven to 350°F (180°C) Gas 4.

Chop the nuts finely. Finely grate rind from orange. Separate the eggs. Whisk the yolks with the sugar in a bowl over a pan of hot water till pale and thick.

Remove from the heat. Add orange rind, breadcrumbs, sifted flour, baking powder, bicarbonate of soda, cinnamon and nuts, and fold in with a metal spoon. Squeeze the orange and add 2 tbsp (2x15 ml) of the juice to the mixture with the sultanas. Whisk the egg whites till stiff but not dry and fold in carefully.

Pour mixture into greased and lined 9 inch (23 cm) springform tin. Bake for about 1 hour till firm and springy to the touch. Cool on a wire rack.

Spicy slab cake

Overall timing 1¼ hours

Freezing Suitable

To serve 12

10 oz	Butter	275 g
10 oz	Caster sugar	275 g
5	Eggs	5
10 oz	Self-raising flour	275 g
1 teasp	Ground ginger	5 ml
1 teasp	Ground cinnamon	5 ml
1 teasp	Grated nutmeg	5 ml
¼ teasp	Ground cloves	1.25 ml
8 oz	Stoned dates	225 g
4 oz	Walnuts	125 g
3 tbsp	Milk	3x15 ml

Preheat the oven to 350°F (180°C) Gas 4.

Cream the butter with the sugar till pale and fluffy. Beat the eggs lightly with a fork, then gradually beat into the creamed mixture. Sift the flour and spices into the bowl, add the chopped dates and walnuts and fold in with a metal spoon, adding the milk to give a soft dropping consistency.

Spread the mixture in a greased and lined 12x9 inch (30x23 cm) tin and smooth the top. Bake for about 45 minutes till firm and a skewer inserted in centre comes out clean. Cool on a wire rack. Cut into squares to serve.

Whisky cake

Overall timing 2 hours plus cooling

Freezing Suitable

To serve 12

4 oz	Seedless raisins	125 g
4 tbsp	Whisky	4x15 ml
4 oz	Candied orange peel	125 g
	Grated rind of 1 orange	
6 oz	Butter	175 g
6 oz	Caster sugar	175 g
3	Eggs	3
4 oz	Plain flour	125 g
4 oz	Self-raising flour	125 g
¼ teasp	Ground cinnamon	1.25 ml

Preheat the oven to 350°F (180°C) Gas 4.

Soak the raisins in the whisky. Chop the candied peel and add to the raisins with the orange rind. Mix well and leave to soak for 10 minutes.

Cream the butter with the sugar till pale and fluffy. Beat the eggs and add, a little at a time, to the creamed mixture, beating well between each addition. Sift the flours and cinnamon over, add the fruit and soaking liquid and fold into the mixture with a metal spoon.

Spread the mixture in a greased and lined 8 inch (20 cm) round cake tin, smooth the surface and make a slight hollow in the centre. Bake for 1¼–1½ hours till a skewer inserted in the cake comes out clean. Allow to cool slightly in the tin, then transfer to a wire rack and leave to cool completely.

Scones

Overall timing 20 minutes

Freezing Not suitable

Makes 8

8 oz	Plain flour	225 g
3 teasp	Baking powder	3x5 ml
	Pinch of salt	
2 oz	Butter	50 g
2 tbsp	Caster sugar	2x15 ml
¼ pint	Milk	150 ml
	Milk or egg for glazing	

Preheat the oven to 450°F (230°C) Gas 8.

Sift flour, baking powder and salt into a mixing bowl. Rub in butter. Add sugar and milk and mix to a soft dough.

Roll out quickly to ½ inch (12.5 mm) thickness on a lightly floured board. Lightly flour scone cutter and cut out scones. Place on lightly floured baking tray and glaze tops with top of the milk or lightly beaten egg. Bake for 10 minutes. Wrap in tea-towel till ready to serve.

Variation

Peel, core and grate 1 dessert apple and scatter over rolled-out dough. Fold in half and press firmly together. Cut and bake as above.

Gingerbread

Overall timing 1¼ hours

Freezing Suitable

Makes 9

8 oz	Plain flour	225 g
1 teasp	Bicarbonate of soda	5 ml
1½ teasp	Ground ginger	7.5 ml
2 oz	Black treacle	50 g
4 oz	Golden syrup	125 g
3 oz	Butter	75 g
2 oz	Soft brown sugar	50 g
2	Eggs	2
2 tbsp	Milk	2x15 ml

Preheat the oven to 325°F (170°C) Gas 3.

Sift flour, soda and ginger into a bowl. Place treacle and golden syrup in a saucepan with butter and brown sugar. Heat till melted.

Beat eggs and milk. Add with melted ingredients to dry ingredients. Mix to a thick batter. Pour into a greased and lined 7 inch (18 cm) square tin. Bake for 1 hour.

Cherry and lemon loaf

Overall timing 1½ hours

Freezing Suitable

To serve 16

8 oz	Self-raising flour	225 g
	Pinch of salt	
4 oz	Butter	125 g
4 oz	Caster sugar	125 g
	Grated rind of 1 lemon	
1	Egg	1
4 fl oz	Milk	120 ml
4 oz	Glacé cherries	125 g

Preheat the oven to 350°F (180°C) Gas 4.

Sift all but 1 tbsp (15 ml) of flour and the salt into a bowl. Rub in butter until mixture resembles fine breadcrumbs. Stir in sugar and lemon rind. Make a well in centre and break in egg. Mix together, adding enough milk to give a soft consistency that won't drop unless flicked from the spoon. Coat cherries in reserved flour and fold into mixture.

Pour into greased and lined 2 lb (900 g) loaf tin and smooth surface. Bake for 45 minutes. Cover with greaseproof and bake for further 30 minutes. Cool on a wire rack.

Sultana loaf cake

Overall timing 1½ hours

Freezing Suitable

To serve 16

8 oz	Self-raising flour	225 g
	Salt	
1 teasp	Ground ginger	5 ml
4 oz	Butter	125 g
2 oz	Caster sugar	50 g
6 oz	Sultanas	175 g
2 tbsp	Clear honey	2x15 ml
1	Egg	1
7 tbsp	Milk	7x15 ml

Preheat the oven to 350°F (180°C) Gas 4.

Sift the flour, a pinch of salt and the ginger into a large bowl. Rub in butter till the mixture resembles fine breadcrumbs. Stir in the sugar and sultanas. Make a well in the centre and add the honey, egg and half the milk. Mix together, adding the remaining milk if necessary to give a soft dropping consistency.

Spread the mixture in a greased and lined 2 lb (900 g) loaf tin and smooth the surface. Bake for 45 minutes. Cover the top lightly with foil and bake for a further 30 minutes till the loaf is springy when lightly pressed. Cool on a wire rack.

Christmas cake

Overall timing Cake: 2–2½ hours. Icing: 30 minutes plus 24 hours standing

Freezing Not suitable

1¼ lb	Mixed dried fruit	600 g
2 oz	Candied peel	50 g
6 oz	Dark brown sugar	175 g
3 tbsp	Golden syrup	3x15 ml
4 oz	Butter	125 g
6 oz	Self-raising flour	175 g
6 oz	Plain flour	175 g
2 teasp	Bicarbonate of soda	2x5 ml
2 teasp	Mixed spice	2x5 ml
2	Large eggs	2
3 tbsp	Apricot jam	3x15 ml
12 oz	Almond paste	350 g
2	Egg whites	2
1 lb	Icing sugar	450 g
2 teasp	Lemon juice	2x5 ml
1 teasp	Glycerine	5 ml

Put fruit in saucepan with peel, sugar, syrup, butter and 8 fl oz (220 ml) water. Bring to the boil, then simmer for 3 minutes. Turn into a bowl and cool.

Preheat the oven to 325°F (170°C) Gas 3.

Sift flours, soda and spice three times, then add to fruit mixture. Beat in eggs. Place in greased and lined 8 inch (20 cm) cake tin, making a slight depression in centre. Bake for about 1½–2 hours or till skewer inserted in centre comes out clean. Cool in tin.

To decorate cake, brush top and sides with warmed apricot jam. Roll out almond paste and use to cover top and sides. Smooth all seams.

Whisk egg whites to a fairly stiff foam. Gradually beat in sifted icing sugar and lemon juice. When icing forms little peaks when lifted up with a knife blade, mix in glycerine. Cover bowl and leave for 24 hours.

Beat icing gently. Spread over cake, flicking up into peaks with a knife blade. Leave to set for a week before cutting.

Honey spice loaf

Overall timing 1 hour 20 minutes

Freezing Suitable

To serve 16

4 oz	Caster sugar	125 g
5 tbsp	Water	5 x 15 ml
8 oz	Honey	225 g
8 oz	Rye flour	225 g
	Salt	
1½ teasp	Bicarbonate of soda	7.5 ml
¼ teasp	Ground cloves	1.25 ml
½ teasp	Ground cinnamon	2.5 ml
¼ teasp	Ground mace	1.25 ml
2 teasp	Ground aniseed	2 x 5 ml
4 tbsp	Ground almonds	4 x 15 ml
½ teasp	Almond essence	2.5 ml
4 oz	Glacé fruits	125 g

Preheat the oven to 325°F (170°C) Gas 3.

Put the sugar and water into a saucepan and heat gently till sugar is dissolved. Pour into a large bowl, add the honey and beat for 2 minutes. Sift the flour, a pinch of salt, the bicarbonate of soda and spices into the mixture. Add the almonds and essence and beat for 4–5 minutes.

Cut the glacé fruits into pieces and stir into the mixture. Spread in a greased and lined 2 lb (900 g) loaf tin and smooth the top. Bake for about 55 minutes till a skewer inserted in the centre comes out clean. Cool in the tin for 10 minutes, then turn out on to a wire rack and leave to cool completely. Cut into slices to serve.

Golden fruit cake

Overall timing 2 hours

Freezing Suitable

To serve 8–10

4 oz	Butter	125 g
4 oz	Caster sugar	125 g
2	Eggs	2
8 oz	Self-raising flour	225 g
	Pinch of salt	
2 oz	Glacé cherries	50 g
3 oz	Sultanas	75 g
2 oz	Candied peel	50 g
1–2 tbsp	Water	1–2 x 15 ml

Preheat the oven to 400°F (200°C) Gas 6.

Cream butter with sugar till light and fluffy. Add the eggs, one at a time, beating between each addition. Stir in the flour, salt, fruit and peel. Mix well, then add enough water to make a soft, but not sticky, dough.

Pour mixture into greased and lined 1 lb (450 g) loaf tin. Bake for 30 minutes, then lower oven temperature to 350°F (180°C) Gas 4 and bake for a further 1 hour. Cover with a piece of foil if the top begins to turn brown too quickly. Cool on a wire rack.

Walnut and orange cake

Overall timing 1 hour 50 minutes

Freezing Suitable

6 oz	Butter	175 g
6 oz	Caster sugar	175 g
3	Eggs	3
	Grated rind of ½ orange	
8 oz	Plain flour	225 g
1½ teasp	Baking powder	7.5 ml
	Pinch of salt	
2 tbsp	Orange juice	2x15 ml
2 oz	Walnuts	50 g

Preheat the oven to 325°F (170°C) Gas 3.

Cream the butter with the sugar till pale and fluffy. Add the beaten eggs, a little at a time, beating well after each addition. Stir in the grated orange rind. Sift in the flour, baking powder and salt and fold in alternately with the orange juice. When the mixture is smooth and will flick easily from a spoon, fold in the chopped walnuts.

Put into a greased and lined 7 inch (18 cm) round cake tin. Bake for 1¼–1½ hours, or until a skewer inserted in the cake comes out clean.

Swiss roll

Overall timing 30 minutes plus cooling

Freezing Suitable: fill after thawing

Makes 2

3	Large eggs	3
3 oz	Caster sugar	75 g
¼ teasp	Vanilla essence	1.25 ml
3 oz	Plain flour	75 g
	Pinch of salt	
1 tbsp	Warm water	15 ml
4 tbsp	Jam	4x15 ml

Preheat the oven to 400°F (200°C) Gas 6.

Separate the eggs. Whisk yolks with the sugar and vanilla in a bowl over a pan of hot water till mixture forms trails when beaters are lifted. Remove from heat. Sift flour and fold into mixture.

Whisk the whites with salt till mixture forms soft peaks that curl downwards. Fold into yolk mixture with a metal spoon, then fold in warm water. Place mixture in greased and lined Swiss roll tin, spreading to sides. Bake for 12–15 minutes till sides of sponge shrink a little.

Turn out sponge on to sheet of greaseproof paper sprinkled with caster sugar. Carefully peel away paper from sponge. Trim edges of sponge with a sharp knife.

Working quickly, spread jam over sponge. With the help of the greaseproof, roll up sponge away from you. Place seam-side down on wire rack to cool.

Orange and almond sponge

Overall timing 1 hour plus cooling

Freezing Suitable: ice after thawing

To serve 10

1	Large orange	1
5	Eggs	5
5 oz	Caster sugar	150 g
3½ oz	Self-raising flour	100 g
	Pinch of salt	
¼ teasp	Ground ginger	1.25 ml
½ teasp	Ground cinnamon	2.5 ml
5 oz	Ground almonds	150 g
	Almond essence	
5 oz	Icing sugar	150 g
1 tbsp	Curaçao	15 ml

Preheat the oven to 400°F (200°C) Gas 6.

Grate the rind from the orange and squeeze out the juice. Separate the eggs. Whisk egg yolks with the sugar till the mixture is pale and thick. Sift the flour, salt and spices over the mixture and add the ground almonds, three drops of essence, orange rind and 3 tbsp (3x15 ml) of the orange juice. Fold in gently.

Whisk the egg whites till stiff and fold into the mixture with a metal spoon. Carefully pour mixture into a greased and lined 9 inch (23 cm) cake tin and smooth the surface. Bake for about 35 minutes till springy to the touch. Cool on a wire rack.

Sift the icing sugar into a bowl and add the Curaçao and 1 tbsp (15 ml) of the remaining orange juice to make an icing that will coat the back of the spoon. Pour the icing on to the top of the cake. Lift the wire rack and tap it several times on the working surface so that the icing flows over the cake and trickles down the sides. Leave to set.

Lemon and cardamom cake

Overall timing $1\frac{1}{4}$–$1\frac{1}{2}$ hours

Freezing Suitable

To serve 8

8 oz	Self-raising flour	225 g
1 teasp	Ground cardamom	5 ml
4 oz	Butter	125 g
4 oz	Caster sugar	125 g
1	Lemon	1
1	Egg	1
2 tbsp	Milk	2x15 ml
1 oz	Flaked almonds	25 g
$\frac{1}{2}$ teasp	Ground cinnamon	2.5 ml

Preheat the oven to 350°F (180°C) Gas 4.

Sift flour and cardamom into a large bowl. Rub in the butter till mixture resembles fine breadcrumbs. Stir in all but 1 teasp (5 ml) of the sugar. Grate the lemon rind and squeeze out the juice. Add both to bowl with the egg. Gradually mix ingredients, adding enough milk to give a soft consistency that won't drop unless flicked from the spoon.

Put mixture into greased and lined 7 inch (18 cm) round cake tin and smooth the surface. Mix together the almonds, cinnamon and reserved sugar and sprinkle over cake. Bake for 1–$1\frac{1}{4}$ hours till cake comes away from the sides. Cool in tin for a few minutes, then turn out on to a wire rack and cool completely.

Nutty honey cake

Overall timing 1 hour

Freezing Not suitable

To serve 8–10

6 oz	Butter	175 g
3 oz	Clear honey	75 g
5 oz	Plain flour	150 g
5 oz	Wholemeal flour	150 g
Filling		
4 oz	Mixed nuts	125 g
2 oz	Sultanas	50 g
1 teasp	Ground cinnamon	5 ml
	Clear honey	

Preheat the oven to 350°F (180°C) Gas 4.

Cream butter with honey till light and fluffy. Mix in sifted flours to make a dough. Roll out half dough on a floured surface and press into greased and lined 7 inch (18 cm) round tin.

Chop nuts and mix with sultanas and cinnamon. Bind with honey. Spread filling over dough in tin.

Roll out remaining dough and cover filling. Press edges to seal. Bake for 30–40 minutes till golden. Cool in the tin.

Lemon shortcake

Overall timing 1 hour

Freezing Suitable

To serve 8

1	Lemon	1
8 oz	Plain flour	225 g
	Salt	
3 oz	Caster sugar	75 g
3 oz	Butter	75 g
1	Egg	1

Preheat the oven to 375°F (190°C) Gas 5.

Grate the rind of the lemon and squeeze out the juice. Sift the flour and a pinch of salt into a mixing bowl and stir in the sugar. Add the melted butter, egg, grated lemon rind and 2 tbsp (2x15 ml) lemon juice. Mix well and knead lightly until the mixture is smooth.

Roll out on a floured surface to fit a greased 8 inch (20 cm) sandwich tin or flan ring. Bake for 20 minutes till golden. Cool in the tin.

Italian nut and honey cake

Overall timing 1 hour

Freezing Not suitable

To serve 10

6 oz	Almonds	175 g
4 oz	Walnuts	125 g
8 oz	Chopped mixed peel	225 g
¼ teasp	Ground allspice	1.25 ml
½ teasp	Ground cinnamon	2.5 ml
1 teasp	Ground coriander	5 ml
5 oz	Plain flour	150 g
4 oz	Icing sugar	125 g
1 tbsp	Water	15 ml
5 oz	Clear honey	150 g

Preheat the oven to 425°F (220°C) Gas 7.

Spread the nuts on a baking tray and toast in the oven till golden. Remove from oven and roughly chop. Reduce oven temperature to 375°F (190°C) Gas 5.

Add chopped mixed peel, spices and flour to nuts and mix well together.

Reserve 1 tbsp (15 ml) of the icing sugar and put the rest in a heavy-based pan with the water and honey. Stir constantly over a low heat until bubbles appear on the surface. Remove from heat immediately. Gradually stir nut and fruit mixture into the syrup.

Turn into 8 inch (20 cm) loose-bottomed flan tin lined with rice paper and smooth surface with a wet knife blade. Sprinkle with reserved icing sugar. Bake for about 30 minutes. Mark into 10 portions and leave to cool in tin before cutting.

Moist date and ginger cake

Overall timing 1¼ hours

Freezing Suitable

To serve 12

8 oz	Stoned dates	225 g
1 teasp	Bicarbonate of soda	5 ml
¼ pint	Boiling water	150 ml
4 oz	Butter	125 g
4 oz	Soft dark brown sugar	125 g
2 tbsp	Black treacle	2x15 ml
1 tbsp	Golden syrup	15 ml
2	Eggs	2
8 oz	Self-raising flour	225 g
2 teasp	Ground ginger	2x5 ml
2 tbsp	Icing sugar	2x15 ml

Preheat the oven to 350°F (180°C) Gas 4.

Chop the dates and place in a small bowl. Sprinkle with bicarbonate of soda, then pour on the boiling water. Leave to cool.

Cream the butter with the sugar till light and fluffy. Beat in the black treacle and syrup, then the eggs, one at a time, beating well. Sift in the flour and ginger, and add the dates and soaking liquid. Stir till well blended.

Pour into a greased and lined 9 inch (23 cm) round cake tin. Bake for 50–60 minutes till the centre of the cake springs back when lightly pressed. Cool on a wire rack. Dredge with icing sugar before serving.

Marble ring cake

Overall timing 1½ hours

Freezing Suitable

To serve 10

4 oz	Butter	125 g
5 oz	Caster sugar	150 g
3	Eggs	3
7 oz	Self-raising flour	200 g
5 tbsp	Milk	5 x 15 ml
1 oz	Cocoa powder	25 g

Preheat the oven to 350°F (180°C) Gas 4.

Cream the butter with the sugar till mixture is pale and fluffy. Beat in the eggs, one at a time. Divide the mixture into two. Sift 4 oz (125 g) of the flour into one-half and fold in with 3 tbsp (3x15 ml) of the milk.

Sift the rest of the flour and the cocoa into the other half of the mixture and fold in with the remaining milk.

Spread a little of the plain mixture over the bottom and sides of a greased and floured 7½ inch (19 cm) ring mould. Carefully spread a thin layer of the chocolate mixture over the plain layer. Repeat the careful layering until both mixtures are used up.

Bake for 1 hour till well risen and firm to the touch. Cool cake slightly in the mould before turning out on to a wire rack to cool completely.

Fresh cherry cake

Overall timing 1½ hours

Freezing Suitable

To serve 8

6	Digestive biscuits	6
1¾ lb	Fresh cherries	750 g
3 oz	Ground almonds	75 g
9 oz	Caster sugar	250 g
½ teasp	Ground cinnamon	2.5 ml
5	Eggs	5
2 tbsp	Kirsch	2x15 ml
1	Lemon	1
4 oz	Plain flour	125 g

Preheat the oven to 350°F (180°C) Gas 4.

Crush the biscuits and sprinkle over the bottom and sides of an oiled 10 inch (25 cm) cake tin.

Stone cherries. Arrange over the bottom of the coated cake tin.

Mix together the almonds, 2 oz (50 g) of the sugar and the cinnamon. Separate the eggs. Beat together the egg yolks, remaining sugar, Kirsch and grated rind and juice of the lemon. Stir in the almond mixture, then fold in the flour lightly. Whisk the egg whites till stiff and fold into the cake mixture using a metal spoon.

Spread the cake mixture over the cherries. Bake for 1 hour 10 minutes. Cool on a wire rack. Dredge with icing sugar before serving.

Hazelnut and honey cake

Overall timing 1¼ hours

Freezing Suitable

To serve 8

6 oz	Butter	175 g
4 oz	Light brown sugar	125 g
4 tbsp	Clear honey	4x15 ml
2	Whole eggs	2
2	Egg yolks	2
8 oz	Wholemeal self-raising flour	225 g
	Pinch of salt	
4 oz	Toasted hazelnuts	125 g
4 tbsp	Milk	4x15 ml

Preheat the oven to 350°F (180°C) Gas 4.

Cream the butter with the sugar and honey, then beat in the whole eggs and yolks. Fold in sifted flour, salt and chopped hazelnuts alternately with the milk.

Put mixture into a greased and lined 7 inch (18 cm) round cake tin. Bake for 1 hour until springy to the touch. Cool on wire rack. Coat with a fudgy icing if a more elaborate cake is desired.

Coffee ring cake

Overall timing 1½ hours

Freezing Suitable

To serve 16

5 oz	Butter	150 g
5 oz	Caster sugar	150 g
	Salt	
2	Large eggs	2
1	Orange	1
3 teasp	Instant coffee powder	3x5 ml
5 oz	Self-raising flour	150 g
¼ teasp	Ground cinnamon	1.25 ml
2 oz	Plain chocolate	50 g
Icing		
6 oz	Icing sugar	175 g
2 teasp	Instant coffee powder	2x5 ml
1 teasp	Cocoa	5 ml
2 tbsp	Hot water	2x15 ml
	Vanilla essence	

Preheat the oven to 325°F (170°C) Gas 3.

Cream butter with sugar and a pinch of salt till light and fluffy. Add eggs one at a time and beat well. Grate orange and add rind to bowl. Squeeze orange and mix 3 tbsp (3x15 ml) juice with the instant coffee. Sift flour and cinnamon and mix into the creamed mixture alternately with the orange/coffee mixture. Grate chocolate and fold in.

Spoon mixture into greased 8½ inch (22 cm) ring mould. Bake for 40–50 minutes. Cool on a wire rack.

To make the icing, sift icing sugar into bowl. Dissolve coffee and cocoa in hot water, then add to icing sugar with a few drops of vanilla essence and mix well. Pour over cooled cake and smooth surface with a knife.

Fatless sponge cake

Overall timing 1½ hours

Freezing Not suitable

To serve 8–10

4	Eggs	4
5 oz	Caster sugar	150 g
½ teasp	Vanilla essence	2.5 ml
2 oz	Plain flour	50 g
2 oz	Potato flour	50 g
1	Egg white	1

Preheat the oven to 350°F (180°C) Gas 4.

Separate eggs. Whisk the yolks with the sugar and vanilla essence in a bowl over a pan of hot water till mixture leaves a trail lasting 20 seconds when the beaters are lifted. Remove from the heat. Add the sifted flours and fold in with a wooden spatula or metal spoon.

Whisk egg whites till stiff. Add about one-quarter of the whites to the yolk mixture and stir in, then fold mixture into the remaining egg white with a metal spoon.

Turn mixture into greased and floured 9 inch (23 cm) fluted tin. Bake for 50 minutes to 1 hour or until top springs back when lightly pressed.

Yogurt cake

Overall timing 2 hours

Freezing Suitable

To serve 10

5 oz	Carton of natural yogurt	141 g
10 oz	Caster sugar	275 g
10 oz	Plain flour	275 g
1 tbsp	Baking powder	15 ml
	Salt	
2	Eggs	2
5 tbsp	Corn oil	5x15 ml
2 tbsp	Rum	2x15 ml
1 tbsp	Icing sugar	15 ml

Preheat the oven to 350°F (180°C) Gas 4.

Pour the yogurt into a large bowl and beat in the sugar. Sift the flour and baking powder with a pinch of salt. Beat together the eggs, oil and rum and add to the yogurt alternately with the flour mixture, beating till smooth.

Pour the mixture into a greased and lined 7 inch (18 cm) round cake tin. Bake for $1\frac{3}{4}$ hours, covering the top lightly with foil after 45 minutes, till a skewer inserted in the centre comes out clean. Cool on a wire rack.

Sift the icing sugar over the cake and mark the top into 10 slices. Serve with cherry jam.

Battenberg cake

Overall timing 1½ hours plus cooling

Freezing Suitable: add almond paste after thawing

To serve 10

8 oz	Butter	225 g
8 oz	Caster sugar	225 g
4	Eggs	4
8 oz	Self-raising flour	225 g
4 tbsp	Milk	4x15 ml
	Red food colouring	
3 tbsp	Apricot jam	3x15 ml
8 oz	Almond paste	225 g

Preheat the oven to 375°F (190°C) Gas 5. Grease and line Swiss roll tin, making pleat in paper down centre to divide in half lengthways.

Cream butter with sugar. Beat in eggs. Sift flour and fold into creamed mixture with milk. Spread half mixture into one side of tin. Add a few drops of food colouring to remaining mixture and spread into other half of tin. Bake for about 45 minutes.

Cut each cake in half lengthways. Warm jam and use to stick cake pieces together in chequerboard pattern. Spread jam over cake. Sprinkle caster sugar over working surface, roll out almond paste and wrap round cake. Crimp edges and make diamond pattern on top using a sharp knife.

Coffee cream torte

Overall timing 1½ hours plus chilling

Freezing Suitable: add cream after thawing

To serve 12

2 teasp	Instant coffee powder	2x5 ml
4	Large eggs	4
5 oz	Caster sugar	150 g
	Pinch of salt	
4 oz	Plain flour	125 g
2 oz	Butter	50 g
¼ pint	Strong black coffee	150 ml
2 tbsp	Rum or Tia Maria	2x15 ml
½ pint	Double cream	284 ml
1 oz	Icing sugar	25 g
12	Chocolate truffles	12

Preheat the oven to 375°F (190°C) Gas 5.

Dissolve coffee in 1 tbsp (15 ml) water in a bowl placed over a pan of hot water. Add eggs, 4 oz (125 g) sugar and salt and whisk till thick. Remove bowl from pan. Sift flour and fold in alternately with melted butter. Pour into greased and lined 8 inch (20 cm) cake tin and bake for 40 minutes.

Dissolve remaining sugar in black coffee and stir in rum or Tia Maria. Spoon over cake, then cool and chill.

Whip cream with icing sugar till stiff. Turn out cake on to serving plate. Spread over half cream. Decorate with remaining cream and truffles.

Grape gâteau

Overall timing 40 minutes plus chilling

Freezing Suitable: decorate with almonds and cream after thawing

To serve 6–8

1	Fatless sponge cake (see page 42)	1
5 oz	Caster sugar	150 g
3 fl oz	Water	90 ml
2 tbsp	Cointreau	2x15 ml
8 oz	Cream cheese	225 g
½ teasp	Vanilla essence	2.5 ml
8 oz	Seedless grapes	225 g
2 oz	Toasted almonds	50 g
	Cream to decorate	

Bake cake in 8½ inch (22 cm) tin and cool.

Dissolve 4 oz (125 g) sugar in water and bring to the boil. Add Cointreau and cool. Cut cake into two layers and place one layer back in tin. Brush generously with syrup.

Beat the cream cheese, remaining sugar and vanilla till smooth. Chop all but eight grapes and fold in. Spread over cake, then place second layer on top and brush with remaining syrup. Cover and chill for several hours.

Remove cake from tin and place on serving plate. Cover top with chopped almonds. Whip cream till stiff and pipe whirls on top of cake. Decorate with reserved whole grapes.

Almond meringue gâteau

Overall timing 1½ hours plus cooling

Freezing Suitable: add buttercream after thawing

To serve 6–8

4	Egg whites	4
3 oz	Ground almonds	75 g
5 oz	Icing sugar	150 g
2 oz	Toasted almonds	50 g
Buttercream		
4	Egg yolks	4
4 oz	Icing sugar	125 g
2 tbsp	Coffee essence	2x15 ml
4 oz	Softened butter	125 g

Preheat the oven to 250°F (130°C) Gas ½.

Whisk egg whites till stiff. Fold in ground almonds and sifted icing sugar.

Place three greased 10 inch (25 cm) flan rings on baking trays covered with non-stick paper. Spread one-third of meringue in each ring. Bake for about 1 hour till crisp and dry. Cool before lifting off flan rings.

To make buttercream, whisk yolks and icing sugar in a bowl placed over a pan of hot water till fluffy. Stir in coffee essence and continue whisking till thick. Remove from heat. Cool, then gradually beat in softened butter.

Sandwich meringue rounds together with two-thirds of buttercream and spread remainder on top. Sprinkle over chopped toasted almonds.

Special honey sponge

Overall timing 35 minutes plus cooling

Freezing Suitable: fill and decorate after thawing

To serve 8

7 oz	Self-raising flour	200 g
1 oz	Cornflour	25 g
½ teasp	Baking powder	2.5 ml
3 oz	Icing sugar	75 g
4 oz	Butter	125 g
4 oz	Caster sugar	125 g
1 tbsp	Clear honey	15 ml
2	Large eggs	2
4 fl oz	Milk	120 ml
3 oz	Nuts	75 g
Filling and decoration		
2 oz	Butter	50 g
4 oz	Icing sugar	125 g
1 tbsp	Clear honey	15 ml
1 tbsp	Warm water	15 ml
2 oz	Blanched almonds and walnuts	50 g
4 fl oz	Carton of double cream	113 ml

Preheat the oven to 350°F (180°C) Gas 4.

Sift flour, cornflour, baking powder and icing sugar together. Cream butter with caster sugar and honey. Beat in eggs, then fold in flour mixture alternately with milk. Stir in chopped nuts. Divide between two greased 7 inch (18 cm) sandwich tins. Bake for 20 minutes. Cool on wire rack.

To make the filling, cream butter with icing sugar, honey and water. Spread on one cake, sprinkle with most of the chopped nuts, then place second cake on top. Whip cream until stiff. Spoon into piping bag fitted with large star nozzle and pipe decorative swirls around top of cake. Decorate with rest of nuts.

Praline-topped lemon cake

Overall timing 1½ hours

Freezing Suitable

To serve 8

4 oz	Butter	125 g
5 oz	Caster sugar	150 g
4	Eggs	4
5 oz	Plain flour	150 g
3 oz	Cornflour	75 g
2 teasp	Baking powder	2x5 ml
2 tbsp	Grated lemon rind	2x15 ml
2 oz	Almonds	50 g
Buttercream		
5 oz	Butter	150 g
5 oz	Icing sugar	150 g
1	Egg yolk	1
2 tbsp	Lemon juice	2x15 ml

Preheat the oven to 350°F (180°C) Gas 4.

Cream butter with 4 oz (125 g) sugar till light and fluffy. Separate eggs and beat egg yolks into creamed mixture. Sift flour, cornflour and baking powder together and fold into creamed mixture with lemon rind. Whisk egg whites till stiff and fold in.

Pour into greased and lined 8 inch (20 cm) cake tin and smooth surface. Bake for 50–60 minutes till top springs back when lightly pressed. Cool on wire rack.

Melt remaining sugar with 1 teasp (5 ml) water in a heavy-based saucepan. Boil until caramelized to a pale golden colour. Add chopped almonds and mix well. Spread on to a greased baking tray. Allow to cool and set hard, then break praline into tiny pieces with a rolling-pin.

To make buttercream, cream butter with sifted icing sugar till soft, then beat in egg yolk and lemon juice.

Cut cake into three layers and sandwich together with most of buttercream. Spread remainder on top and lightly press in praline.

Banana and walnut gâteau

Overall timing 1 hour plus cooling

Freezing Not suitable

To serve 8–10

4	Large eggs	4
6 oz	Caster sugar	175 g
2 tbsp	Warm water	2x15 ml
4 oz	Plain flour	125 g
1 teasp	Baking powder	5 ml
2 tbsp	Milk	2x15 ml
2 oz	Butter	50 g
$\frac{1}{2}$ pint	Carton of double cream	284 ml
5	Large bananas	5
	Chopped walnuts	
	Walnut halves	

Preheat the oven to 375°F (190°C) Gas 5.

Separate eggs. Beat yolks with sugar and water till light and fluffy. Sift flour with baking powder and add to yolk mixture alternately with milk. Melt butter and add.

Whisk egg whites till stiff and fold into mixture. Spoon into a greased and lined 8 inch (20 cm) round deep cake tin. Bake for 30–35 minutes. Cool on a wire rack.

Whip the cream till thick. Peel and slice the bananas.

Cut the cake into three layers. Sandwich back together with most of the cream and banana slices and the chopped walnuts. Decorate the top with the rest of the cream and bananas and walnut halves. Serve immediately.

Christening cake

Overall timing 3 hours plus overnight chilling

Freezing Suitable: fill and ice after thawing

To serve 30

12	Eggs	12
12 oz	Caster sugar	350 g
14 oz	Plain flour	400 g
2 oz	Butter	50 g
4 oz	Ground almonds	125 g
1 lb	Sugared almonds	450 g
	Silver balls	
Filling		
5	Egg yolks	5
9 oz	Granulated sugar	250 g
5 tbsp	Water	5x15 ml
12 oz	Unsalted butter	350 g
Icing		
1 lb	Icing sugar	450 g
2	Egg whites	2

Preheat the oven to 375°F (190°C) Gas 5.

Make cake mixture in two batches. Beat half eggs and sugar till thick and pale. Sift half flour and fold into egg mixture with half melted butter and almonds. Pour into greased and lined sandwich tins, one 6 inch (15 cm) and one 10 inch (25 cm). Bake for 15–20 minutes for small cake and 30 minutes for large cake. Cool on a wire rack. Make second batch and bake in 7 inch (18 cm) tin and 9 inch (22 cm) tin, allowing 30–35 minutes.

To make filling, put egg yolks into a bowl and whisk well. Dissolve sugar in water in a saucepan. Boil for 2–3 minutes, without allowing it to colour. Pour hot syrup on to egg yolks, beating continuously. Cool, then gradually work in softened butter. Use to sandwich cake layers together and to secure cakes on top of each other, largest on bottom. Chill overnight.

To make icing, sift icing sugar into a large bowl, add egg whites and beat well. Add 1–2 tbsp (1–2x15 ml) hot water to give a coating consistency. Coat the entire cake with icing. Place on a serving dish. Decorate with sugared almonds and silver balls.

Mocha gâteau

Overall timing 1¼ hours

Freezing Suitable

To serve 12

2 teasp	Instant coffee	2x5 ml
4	Large eggs	4
4 oz	Caster sugar	125 g
4 oz	Plain flour	125 g
2 oz	Butter	50 g
2 oz	Milk chocolate flake	50 g
Filling and topping		
1 tbsp	Cornflour	15 ml
¼ pint	Milk	150 ml
3 tbsp	Caster sugar	3x15 ml
1 tbsp	Instant coffee	15 ml
1	Egg yolk	1
6 oz	Butter	175 g
3 oz	Icing sugar	75 g

Preheat the oven to 375°F (190°C) Gas 5.

Dissolve coffee in 1 tbsp (15 ml) water in large bowl over pan of hot water. Add eggs, sugar and pinch of salt and whisk till very thick. Remove bowl from pan. Sift flour and fold in alternately with melted butter. Pour into greased and lined 8 inch (20 cm) cake tin. Bake for 40 minutes. Cool on a wire rack.

To make filling, place cornflour in small saucepan and blend in milk. Add sugar and coffee and bring to the boil, stirring. Simmer for 2–3 minutes, stirring constantly. Remove from heat and cool slightly, then add egg yolk and beat well. Cook over gentle heat for 2 minutes, then remove from heat and leave to cool.

Beat butter with sifted icing sugar. Add cooled custard and beat to a smooth creamy consistency.

Cut sponge into two layers and sandwich back together with one-third of filling. Coat cake with remainder and decorate with crumbled flake.

Refrigerator coffee cake

Overall timing 1½ hours

Freezing Suitable

To serve 12

6 oz	Butter	175 g
6 oz	Caster sugar	175 g
1 teasp	Vanilla essence	5 ml
3	Eggs	3
8 oz	Self-raising flour	225 g
	Pinch of salt	
4 tbsp	Milk	4x15 ml
12	Sugar coffee beans	12
1 oz	Flaked almonds	25 g
Coffee cream		
4	Eggs	4
10 oz	Granulated sugar	275 g
14 oz	Butter	400 g
2 tbsp	Coffee essence	2x15 ml

Preheat the oven to 350°F (180°C) Gas 4.

Cream butter with sugar till light and fluffy. Beat in vanilla essence and eggs. Sift flour and salt and add to mixture alternately with milk. Pour into greased and lined 2 lb (900 g) loaf tin. Bake for 35 minutes. Cool on a wire rack.

Lightly beat eggs in a saucepan. Add sugar and heat very gently till sugar has dissolved. Remove from heat and allow to cool, stirring occasionally. Cream butter, then gradually beat in cold egg mixture and coffee essence.

Cut the sponge cake into three layers and sandwich back together with some of the cream. Place cake on a piece of foil on a plate and coat top and sides with cream, saving a little for decoration. Chill for at least 1 hour till cream is firm.

Slide cake off foil onto plate. Mark with ridges, using a fork. Decorate with remaining cream, coffee beans and almonds.

Chocolate pistachio gâteau

Overall timing 1 hour plus chilling

Freezing Not suitable

To serve 10

12 oz	Plain flour	350 g
	Pinch of salt	
9 oz	Butter	250 g
5 oz	Sugar	150 g
2	Egg yolks	2
Filling		
4 oz	Shelled pistachios	125 g
4	Egg whites	4
7 oz	Caster sugar	200 g
4 oz	Ground almonds	125 g
	Grated rind of $\frac{1}{2}$ lemon	
1 tbsp	Rum	15 ml
2 oz	Milk chocolate	50 g

Sift the flour and salt into a bowl and rub in the fat till the mixture resembles fine breadcrumbs. Stir in the sugar and egg yolks and mix to a soft dough. Chill for 30 minutes.

Preheat the oven to 400°F (200°C) Gas 6.

Divide the dough in half. Roll out and use to line two 9 inch (23 cm) sponge tins. Prick bottoms and bake blind for 15 minutes. Cool on a wire rack.

Reserve a few pistachios for decoration; finely chop the rest. Whisk the egg whites till soft peaks form. Gradually whisk in the sugar till the mixture is stiff and glossy. Fold the chopped nuts into the meringue with the ground almonds, grated lemon rind and rum. Spoon into the pastry cases. Place one pastry cake on a baking tray and invert the other on top. Return to the oven and bake for a further 15 minutes. Cool on a wire rack.

Melt the chocolate in a bowl over a pan of hot water. Spread over the top of the cake with a palette knife. Cut the reserved pistachios in half and arrange in a circle around the edge of the cake.

Pear refrigerator cake

Overall timing 45 minutes plus 4 hours chilling

Freezing Not suitable

To serve 6

1 pint	Water	560 ml
2 tbsp	Lemon juice	2x15 ml
3 oz	Granulated sugar	75 g
1	Vanilla pod	1
4	Large firm pears	4
4 oz	Softened butter	125 g
3 oz	Icing sugar	75 g
2 oz	Ground almonds	50 g
7 oz	Nice biscuits	200 g
2 tbsp	Kirsch	2x15 ml
2 oz	Chocolate cake covering	50 g
2 tbsp	Single cream	2x15 ml

Put water, lemon juice, granulated sugar and vanilla pod into a saucepan and heat gently, stirring till sugar dissolves. Bring to the boil. Peel, core and quarter pears and add to the syrup. Simmer gently for 10 minutes till transparent. Remove from the heat and leave to cool in the syrup.

Cream butter with sifted icing sugar and ground almonds. Crush biscuits and add to mixture with the Kirsch.

Lift pears out of syrup and drain on kitchen paper. Reserve syrup. Thinly slice pears and fold into creamed mixture. Spoon into a 2 lb (900 g) loaf tin lined with foil. Smooth top, fold foil in over cake and put a weight on top. Chill for at least 4 hours.

Melt chocolate in a bowl over a pan of hot water. Remove from the heat and stir in 2 tbsp (2x15 ml) pear syrup and the cream.

Remove cake from tin and place on a serving dish. Spread warm chocolate icing over and leave to set.

Cocoa Madeira cake

Overall timing 1 hour 20 minutes

Freezing Suitable

To serve 10

6 oz	Butter	175 g
6 oz	Caster sugar	175 g
3	Eggs	3
4 oz	Self-raising flour	125 g
2 oz	Cocoa powder	50 g
	Pinch of salt	
3 tbsp	Madeira	3 x 15 ml
2 tbsp	Milk	2 x 15 ml
2 oz	Walnuts	50 g

Preheat the oven to 350°F (180°C) Gas 4.

Cream the butter with the sugar till light and fluffy. Beat the eggs and add to creamed mixture a little at a time, beating well after each addition. Sift together the flour, cocoa and salt. Add to creamed mixture a little at a time, alternating with the Madeira and milk. When the mixture is smooth and will flick easily from the spoon, fold in half the chopped walnuts.

Put mixture into greased and lined 7 inch (18 cm) round cake tin and smooth top. Bake for 45 minutes. Sprinkle with remaining walnuts and bake for further 15–20 minutes till skewer inserted into cake comes out clean. Cool on a wire rack.

Frosted walnut cake

Overall timing 1¼ hours plus cooling

Freezing Suitable: fill and ice after thawing

To serve 10

6 oz	White vegetable fat	175 g
12 oz	Caster sugar	350 g
½ teasp	Vanilla essence	2.5 ml
9 oz	Plain flour	250 g
1 tbsp	Baking powder	15 ml
7 fl oz	Milk	200 ml
4	Egg whites	4
Frosting		
1 lb	Cube sugar	450 g
¼ teasp	Cream of tartar	1.25 ml
2	Egg whites	2
½ teasp	Vanilla essence	2.5 ml
2 oz	Chopped walnuts	50 g
10	Walnut halves	10

Preheat the oven to 350°F (180°C) Gas 4.

Cream fat with sugar and vanilla essence till fluffy. Sift flour, baking powder and a pinch of salt together and fold into creamed mixture alternately with milk. Whisk egg whites till stiff and fold in. Divide between three greased and lined 8 inch (20 cm) sandwich tins. Bake for 30–35 minutes. Cool on a wire rack.

To make frosting, put sugar, cream of tartar and 6 fl oz (170 ml) water in a saucepan and stir over a low heat till sugar dissolves. Stop stirring and bring to the boil. Boil to a temperature of 240°F (116°C).

Meanwhile, whisk egg whites till stiff. Pour syrup in a thin stream on to whites, whisking constantly till frosting stands in soft peaks. Whisk in vanilla essence. Fold chopped walnuts into one-quarter of frosting and use to sandwich cakes together. Spread remaining frosting over cake and decorate with walnut halves.

Sachertorte

Overall timing 1½ hours plus cooling

Freezing Not suitable

To serve 8

4 oz	Plain chocolate	125 g
4 oz	Unsalted butter	125 g
6 oz	Caster sugar	175 g
5	Eggs	5
3 oz	Ground almonds	75 g
4 tbsp	Self-raising flour	4x15 ml
½ pint	Carton of double or whipping cream	268 ml
	Hazelnuts	
Icing		
8 oz	Plain chocolate	225 g
4 oz	Butter	125 g

Preheat the oven to 400°F (200°C) Gas 6.
Melt chocolate with butter till smooth. Beat in the sugar. Separate eggs and gradually add yolks to chocolate mixture, beating well. Whisk egg whites till stiff. Gently fold whites into chocolate mixture, followed by ground almonds and flour. Divide mixture between two greased 8 inch (20 cm) sandwich tins and smooth top. Bake for 20–25 minutes. Cool on a wire rack.

Whip half cream till thick and use to sandwich together the cooled cakes.

To make icing, melt chocolate with butter in a bowl placed over a pan of hot water. Leave to cool for 20–30 minutes until of a coating consistency, then spread over top and sides of cake. Whip remaining cream and pipe large swirls around the edge of the cake. Decorate each swirl with a hazelnut.

Chocolate log

Overall timing 40 minutes plus chilling

Freezing Not suitable

To serve 10–12

2	Eggs	2
1½ oz	Caster sugar	40 g
1 oz	Plain flour	25 g
1 oz	Cornflour	25 g
1 oz	Chopped pistachio nuts or angelica	25 g
Filling and icing		
3½ oz	Softened butter	100 g
7 oz	Icing sugar	200 g
7 oz	Plain chocolate cake covering	200 g
2 tbsp	Rum or brandy (optional)	2x15 ml

Preheat the oven to 400°F (200°C) Gas 6.

Separate eggs. Beat whites in a bowl with sugar till stiff peaks form. Beat yolks till pale, then fold into whites. Sift flour and cornflour into mixture and fold in gently. Spread mixture evenly in greased and lined 13½x9½ inch (34x24 cm) Swiss roll tin and bake for 10 minutes till lightly golden. Turn cake out on to tea-towel. Carefully peel off paper and roll up cake enclosing towel. Cool.

Cream butter with sugar. Melt chocolate and beat into creamed mixture with rum or brandy, if using.

Unroll cake and spread with half chocolate mixture. Roll up and place on a serving plate, seam underneath. Cover cake with remaining chocolate mixture. Make marks in chocolate icing with a fork so that it looks like bark. Sprinkle log with chopped pistachio nuts or angelica and chill before serving.

Chocolate ring cake

Overall timing 1½ hours plus cooling

Freezing Suitable: ice and decorate after thawing

To serve 15–20

4 oz	Butter	125 g
5 oz	Caster sugar	150 g
	Pinch of salt	
	Grated rind of 1 lemon	
4	Eggs	4
1 tbsp	Rum	15 ml
5 oz	Plain flour	150 g
2 oz	Cornflour	50 g
1 teasp	Baking powder	5 ml
Chocolate filling		
6 oz	Unsalted butter	175 g
2 oz	Icing sugar	50 g
2 tbsp	Cocoa powder	2x15 ml

Icing and decoration

8 oz	Cooking chocolate	225 g
½ oz	Butter	15 g
1 oz	Nuts	25 g
15–20	Glacé cherries	15–20

Preheat the oven to 350°F (180°C) Gas 4.

Cream butter with sugar, then beat in salt, grated rind, eggs and rum. Sift flour, cornflour and baking powder together and fold into creamed mixture. Spoon into greased 9 inch (23 cm) ring mould and bake for 55 minutes. Cool on a wire rack.

To make the filling, cream butter with sugar and cocoa powder. Cut cake into three or four thin layers and sandwich together with filling, saving some to decorate the top.

Melt chocolate and spread over cake. Melt butter and cook chopped nuts till golden. Sprinkle round the bottom edge of the chocolate. Pipe remaining chocolate filling in swirls on cake. Add cherry to each.

Queen of Sheba cake

Overall timing 2 hours plus cooling

Freezing Suitable

To serve 8

10 oz	Plain chocolate	275 g
6	Eggs	6
9 oz	Butter	250 g
9 oz	Honey	250 g
5 oz	Plain flour	150 g
1 tbsp	Oil	15 ml
4 oz	Hazelnuts	125 g
4 oz	Split almonds	125 g
1 tbsp	Chocolate vermicelli	15 ml
3 tbsp	Icing sugar	3x15 ml

Preheat the oven to 350°F (180°C) Gas 4.

Gently melt 9 oz (250 g) of the chocolate. Separate the eggs. Cream the butter with the honey, then beat in the chocolate and egg yolks. Add sifted flour, oil and chopped nuts and beat well. Whisk the egg whites till stiff and fold into the mixture.

Turn into a greased and lined 9 inch (23 cm) cake tin. Bake for 1½ hours.

Meanwhile, make curls from remaining chocolate: melt chocolate in saucepan and pour on to oiled marble slab or Formica surface. When chocolate has almost set but is not hard, scrape off thin slivers or curls with a knife. Chill.

Cool cake on a wire rack.

Sprinkle chocolate vermicelli over cake, then sift icing sugar around edge. Arrange the chocolate curls in the centre.

Rum and apricot pudding cake

Overall timing 55 minutes

Freezing Not suitable

To serve 6

1 pint	Milk	560 ml
½ teasp	Vanilla essence	2.5 ml
4	Eggs	4
4 tbsp	Caster sugar	4x15 ml
4 oz	Sponge cake	125 g
2 tbsp	Rum	2x15 ml
4 oz	Chopped glacé fruits	125 g
1 oz	Butter	25 g
8 oz	Apricot jam	225 g

Preheat the oven to 375°F (190°C) Gas 5.

Put the milk and vanilla essence into a saucepan and bring to the boil. Meanwhile, separate the eggs. Add the sugar to the yolks and beat together with a fork. Pour the hot milk over the yolks, stirring constantly.

Crumble the sponge cake into a bowl. Strain the custard over the cake and mix in half the rum, the glacé fruits and butter. Leave to cool.

Whisk the egg whites till stiff. Fold into the crumb mixture with a metal spoon. Pour the mixture into a greased and lined 2 pint (1.1 litre) soufflé dish and smooth the top. Bake for about 35–40 minutes till well risen and golden.

Put the apricot jam into a saucepan with remaining rum and heat gently till melted.

Serve the cake hot from the dish, with the apricot sauce separately in a sauceboat. Or, leave the cake to cool completely and turn out on to a serving dish. Pour the hot apricot sauce on top and serve immediately.

Chestnut yule log

Overall timing 25 minutes plus 1 hour setting

Freezing Suitable: decorate after thawing

To serve 8

4 oz	Plain dessert chocolate	125 g
4 oz	Butter	125 g
4 oz	Icing sugar	125 g
1 lb	Can of unsweetened chestnut purée	450 g
	Icing sugar to dredge	

Melt the chocolate in a bowl placed over a saucepan of hot water. Remove bowl from heat and stir in butter, sifted icing sugar and chestnut purée. Mix well to a smooth paste.

Mark a rectangle, 14x7 inches (35x18 cm), on a sheet of foil. Spread chestnut paste evenly within the rectangle. Roll into a log shape, easing foil up and away from paste as it is rolled. Put in refrigerator or freezer to set.

Remove foil and place log on cake board. Mark surface with a fork to represent the bark of the log. Sprinkle with unsifted icing sugar.

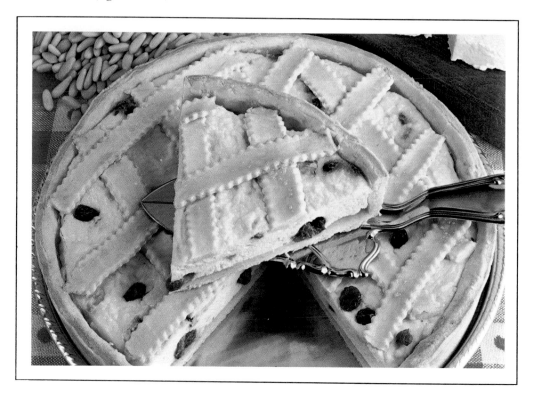

Honey and lemon cheesecake

Overall timing 1¼ hours plus cooling

Freezing Suitable

To serve 12

6 oz	Rich shortcrust pastry	175 g
2	Eggs	2
1 lb	Curd cheese	450 g
6 tbsp	Thick honey	6x15 ml
2	Lemons	2
4 oz	Sultanas	125 g

Preheat the oven to 400°F (200°C) Gas 6.

Roll out dough and use to line 8½ inch (22 cm) loose-bottomed flan tin, reserving any trimmings. Prick bottom. Bake blind for 10 minutes, then remove from oven and reduce temperature to 350°F (180°C) Gas 4.

Separate the eggs. Put the yolks into a bowl with the cheese, honey and the grated rind of one of the lemons. Squeeze juice from both lemons and add to the bowl with the sultanas. Mix well.

In another bowl, whisk the egg whites to soft peaks and fold into the cheese mixture with a metal spoon. Pour into flan case and smooth the surface.

Roll out dough trimmings and cut into thin strips with a pastry wheel. Arrange in a lattice pattern over the filling. Bake for 50–55 minutes till set. Cool in tin, then turn out and serve cold.

Upside-down cheesecake

Overall timing 1¼ hours plus chilling

Freezing Suitable

To serve 8

8 oz	Nice biscuits	225 g
4 oz	Butter	125 g
3 tbsp	Light soft brown sugar	3x15 ml
1 teasp	Ground cinnamon	5 ml
Filling		
12	Petits suisses	12
4 tbsp	Single cream	4x15 ml
4 teasp	Plain flour	4x5 ml
3 oz	Caster sugar	75 g
1 teasp	Vanilla essence	5 ml
1	Lemon	1
4	Eggs	4

Preheat the oven to 350°F (180°C) Gas 4.

Crush biscuits. Put butter, sugar and cinnamon into a saucepan and heat gently till sugar dissolves. Remove from heat and stir in biscuit crumbs. Press all but 4 tbsp (4x15 ml) over bottom and sides of greased 9 inch (23 cm) loose-bottomed flan tin.

Beat cheese with cream, flour, sugar, vanilla essence, grated rind of the lemon and 1 tbsp (15 ml) of the juice. Separate eggs. Beat yolks into the cheese mixture. Whisk whites till stiff and fold into cheese mixture. Pour into crumb case and smooth the top. Sprinkle remaining crumbs on top and press down lightly.

Bake for 45 minutes till set. Switch off the oven, open the door slightly and leave cheesecake in oven till cold. Chill for 2–3 hours, then invert on to a serving dish.

Small cakes and biscuits

Brownies

Overall timing 45 minutes plus cooling

Freezing Suitable

Makes 30

4 oz	Plain dessert chocolate	125 g
4 oz	Unsalted butter	125 g
1 teasp	Vanilla essence	5 ml
4	Eggs	4
$\frac{1}{2}$ teasp	Salt	2.5 ml
14 oz	Caster sugar	400 g
4 oz	Plain flour	125 g
4 oz	Walnuts	125 g

Preheat the oven to 350°F (180°C) Gas 4.

Put chocolate into a bowl with the butter and vanilla essence and place over a pan of simmering water. Stir till melted, then remove bowl from pan and cool.

Whisk eggs and salt till pale and fluffy. Sprinkle the sugar on top and continue whisking till evenly mixed. Fold in the chocolate mixture with a metal spoon, then fold in the sifted flour and coarsely chopped nuts.

Pour into a greased and lined 9x13 inch (23x33 cm) tin and smooth the top. Bake for about 25 minutes till firm. Cool in the tin, then cut into squares. If serving as a dessert top the brownies with whipped cream.

Madeleines with cinnamon

Overall timing 50 minutes plus chilling

Freezing Suitable: bake after thawing

Makes 16

6 oz	Plain flour	175 g
3 oz	Butter	75 g
1 tbsp	Caster sugar	15 ml
1	Egg yolk	1
Filling		
4 oz	Butter	125 g
4 oz	Caster sugar	125 g
2	Eggs	2
2 oz	Ground almonds	50 g
$\frac{1}{4}$ teasp	Almond essence	1.25 ml
4 oz	Self-raising flour	125 g
1 teasp	Ground cinnamon	5 ml
	Milk to mix	
	Apricot jam	
1 tbsp	Icing sugar	15 ml

Sift flour into a bowl and rub in fat. Stir in sugar, egg yolk and enough water to bind to a soft dough. Roll out to $\frac{1}{4}$ inch (6 mm) thickness and use to line two madeleine sheets. Trim the edges and chill for 30 minutes.

Preheat the oven to 375°F (190°C) Gas 5.

To make filling, cream butter with all but 1 tbsp (15 ml) caster sugar. Gradually beat in eggs, then mix in almonds and almond essence. Sift in flour and cinnamon and fold in with enough milk to give a soft dropping consistency.

Put $\frac{1}{2}$ teasp (2.5 ml) jam into each pastry case, then spoon filling into each case. Bake for 15–20 minutes till the filling is golden and springs back when lightly pressed. Cool on a wire rack.

Mix icing sugar and remaining caster sugar together and sift over tartlets before serving.

Date squares

Overall timing 1 hour

Freezing Suitable

Makes 12

1 lb	Stoned dates	450 g
3 tbsp	Water	3x15 ml
1 tbsp	Lemon juice	15 ml
7 oz	Self-raising flour	200 g
1 oz	Bran	25 g
4 oz	Butter	125 g
3 oz	Caster sugar	75 g
1	Egg	1
1 tbsp	Milk	15 ml

Preheat the oven to 350°F (180°C) Gas 4.

Chop dates and place in saucepan with water and lemon juice. Cook, stirring, till mixture is like a paste – about 5 minutes. Leave to cool.

Place flour and bran in mixing bowl. Rub in butter till mixture resembles breadcrumbs. Add 2 oz (50 g) of the sugar. Separate egg. Add yolk and milk to dough and knead till smooth.

Divide dough in half. Press one half over bottom of greased 9 inch (23 cm) square cake tin. Spread with date mixture. Roll out rest of dough and place on dates.

Lightly whisk egg white with a fork. Brush over top and sprinkle with remaining caster sugar. Bake for 30–35 minutes. Cut into squares while hot and leave in tin to cool before serving.

Lemon spice squares

Overall timing 1½ hours

Freezing Suitable

Makes 9

4 oz	Butter	125 g
4 oz	Caster sugar	125 g
	Grated rind of 1 lemon	
2	Eggs	2
2 oz	Chopped candied lemon peel	50 g
4 oz	Plain flour	125 g
2 oz	Ground almonds	50 g
½ teasp	Ground cinnamon	2.5 ml
½ teasp	Ground cloves	2.5 ml
1½ teasp	Baking powder	7.5 ml
2 tbsp	Lemon juice	2 x 15 ml

Preheat the oven to 325°F (170°C) Gas 3.

Cream butter with sugar till light and fluffy. Add lemon rind and beat in the eggs. Stir in the candied lemon peel. Sift together the flour, spices and baking powder and fold into mixture, followed by the almonds and lemon juice.

Turn the mixture into a greased and lined 7 inch (18 cm) square cake tin and smooth the surface. Bake for 1 hour till top springs back when lightly pressed. Cool on a wire rack. Cut into squares to serve.

Hazelnut cakes

Overall timing 1½ hours

Freezing Suitable

Makes 6

3 oz	Finely ground hazelnuts	75 g
2 tbsp	Cornflour	2x15 ml
1 teasp	Baking powder	5 ml
3	Eggs	3
4 oz	Caster sugar	125 g
	Whole hazelnuts	
Filling		
4 oz	Butter	125 g
2 oz	Icing sugar	50 g
2 tbsp	Powdered praline (see page 47)	2x15 ml
1	Egg yolk	1
Icing		
4 oz	Icing sugar	125 g
1 teasp	Instant coffee powder	5 ml
2 teasp	Hot water	2x5 ml

Preheat the oven to 350°F (180°C) Gas 4.

Mix the nuts with cornflour and baking powder. Whisk the eggs and sugar in another bowl over pan of hot water until thick and fluffy. Fold in nut mixture thoroughly but gently. Spread evenly in a greased and lined 7x12 inch (18x30 cm) Swiss roll tin. Bake for 20–30 minutes, or till firm to touch. Remove from tin and allow to cool.

Cut cake into rounds or squares.

To make the filling, beat the butter with the icing sugar until smooth. Add the praline and egg yolk and mix well.

Sift icing sugar into a bowl. Mix in the instant coffee dissolved in hot water. Spread the filling on half the sponges. Top each with a plain sponge. Spread the icing smoothly on top and decorate with a whole hazelnut. Leave to set before serving.

Duchesses

Overall timing 2 hours

Freezing Not suitable

Makes 12

2	Egg whites	2
4 oz	Caster sugar	125 g
2 oz	Ground hazelnuts	50 g
1 oz	Toasted hazelnuts	25 g
2 oz	Plain chocolate	50 g

Preheat the oven to 250°F (130°C) Gas $\frac{1}{2}$.

Whisk the egg whites with half the sugar till stiff. Carefully fold in the ground nuts, then the remaining sugar. Spoon the mixture into a piping bag fitted with a plain wide nozzle. Pipe 1 inch (2.5 cm) wide fingers about 3 inches (7.5 cm) long on to a baking tray lined with rice paper. Sprinkle with chopped toasted hazelnuts and bake for $1\frac{1}{2}$ hours.

Cut paper round fingers with a sharp knife, then remove from tray.

Melt the chocolate. Spread rice-papered sides of half the fingers with chocolate and join to remaining fingers. Leave to set.

Coconut macaroons

Overall timing 1¼ hours

Freezing Not suitable

Makes 15

4 oz	Desiccated coconut	125 g
1 teasp	Vanilla essence	5 ml
	Salt	
¼	Can of condensed milk	¼
2	Egg whites	2
½ teasp	Cream of tartar	2.5 ml

Preheat the oven to 300°F (150°C) Gas 2.

Place coconut, vanilla and a good pinch of salt in mixing bowl. Add condensed milk and mix to firm paste. Whisk egg whites and cream of tartar till stiff, then fold into paste.

Heap small spoonfuls of mixture on to baking tray lined with rice paper, leaving spreading space. Bake for 45 minutes. Turn off oven and leave inside for 15 minutes.

Choc-topped cookies

Overall timing 1 hour

Freezing Not suitable

Makes 55–60

2 oz	Stoned dates	50 g
2 oz	Seedless raisins	50 g
5 oz	Ground hazelnuts	150 g
3 oz	Milk chocolate	75 g
3 oz	Cornflour	75 g
3	Egg whites	3
	Salt	
8 oz	Caster sugar	225 g
4 oz	Plain chocolate cake covering	125 g

Preheat the oven to 350°F (180°C) Gas 4.

Coarsely chop dates and mix with raisins, hazelnuts, grated milk chocolate and cornflour. Beat egg whites with pinch of salt till stiff, then gradually beat in sugar. Fold in chocolate mixture.

With a teaspoon, place small portions on baking trays lined with rice paper, leaving spreading space. Bake for 35 minutes. Cool, then cut paper around biscuits.

Melt plain chocolate and brush over top and sides of biscuits. Leave to set before serving.

Sponge fingers

Overall timing 30 minutes

Freezing Suitable

Makes 16

4	Eggs	4
4 oz	Caster sugar	125 g
1 oz	Cornflour	25 g
3 oz	Plain flour	75 g
	Icing sugar	

Preheat the oven to 375°F (190°C) Gas 5.

Separate the eggs. Whisk whites in a bowl with 2 tbsp (2x15 ml) of the caster sugar till soft peaks form. In another bowl, beat egg yolks with remaining caster sugar. Fold yolks into whites carefully, then gradually fold in the sifted flours.

Put mixture into a piping bag fitted with a plain wide nozzle and pipe fingers 3–4 inches (7.5–10 cm) long on to greased and floured baking trays, spacing them well apart. Dust lightly with sifted icing sugar and bake for 12 minutes. Cool on wire rack.

Spicy raisin biscuits

Overall timing 1 hour plus chilling

Freezing Not suitable

Makes 40

8 oz	Butter	225 g
8 oz	Caster sugar	225 g
1	Egg	1
2 tbsp	Rum	2x15 ml
8 oz	Seedless raisins	225 g
12 oz	Self-raising flour	350 g
	Salt	
½ teasp	Ground cloves	2.5 ml
1 teasp	Ground ginger	5 ml
1	Egg white	1

Cream butter with all but 1 tbsp (15 ml) sugar till pale and fluffy. Gradually beat in egg and rum. Stir in raisins. Sift flour, pinch of salt and spices into mixture and mix to a soft dough. Chill for 30 minutes.

Preheat the oven to 350°F (180°C) Gas 4.

Roll out dough on a floured surface till $\frac{1}{4}$ inch (6 mm) thick. Stamp out rounds with pastry cutter. Arrange on greased baking trays.

Beat egg white and remaining sugar together till frothy and brush over biscuits. Bake for about 15 minutes till pale golden. Cool on the trays for 3–4 minutes till firm, then transfer to a wire rack and leave to cool completely.

Honey galettes

Overall timing 40 minutes plus chilling

Freezing Suitable: refresh in 375°F (190°C) Gas 5 oven for 5 minutes

Makes 8

6 oz	Self-raising flour	175 g
3½ oz	Butter	100 g
2 oz	Thick honey	50 g
1 tbsp	Caster sugar	15 ml
1	Lemon	1
1	Egg	1
	Granulated sugar	

Preheat the oven to 375°F (190°C) Gas 5.

Sift the flour into a mixing bowl. Make a well in the centre and add the softened butter, honey and caster sugar. Grate the rind from the lemon and add to the bowl with 1 tbsp (15 ml) of the juice. Separate the egg and add the yolk to the bowl. Mix well together with a wooden spoon until the mixture forms a ball and leaves the sides of the bowl clean. Chill for 30 minutes.

Divide mixture into eight and roll out each piece on a lightly floured surface to a round about ½ inch (12.5 mm) thick. Place on baking trays.

Whisk egg white lightly and brush over biscuits. Sprinkle each biscuit with 1–2 tbsp (1–2x15 ml) granulated sugar. Bake for about 15 minutes, then remove from trays and cool on wire rack.

Orange liqueur biscuits

Overall timing 45 minutes plus chilling

Freezing Suitable: cut out and bake after thawing

Makes 36

2	Hard-boiled egg yolks	2
8 oz	Plain flour	225 g
4 oz	Caster sugar	125 g
	Salt	
	Ground cinnamon	
4 oz	Butter	125 g
2 tbsp	Orange liqueur	2x15 ml

Push egg yolks through a sieve into a mixing bowl. Sift in the flour and mix well. Make a well in centre and add sugar and a pinch each of salt and cinnamon.

Cut the butter into pieces and work into the mixture, a little at a time. Work in the liqueur and roll paste into a ball. Lightly dust with flour and leave in a cool place (not the refrigerator) for at least 1 hour.

Preheat the oven to 375°F (190°C) Gas 5.

Roll out the paste thinly and stamp out shapes with fancy pastry cutters. Place biscuits on a greased and lined baking tray and bake for 10–15 minutes, till light golden. Remove biscuits carefully from paper and cool on a wire rack.

Almond crescents

Overall timing 30 minutes plus cooling

Freezing Suitable: bake from frozen, allowing 20–25 minutes

Makes 20

5 oz	Blanched almonds	150 g
2 oz	Caster sugar	50 g
	A few drops of vanilla essence	
1	Egg white	1
1 oz	Plain flour	25 g
1	Egg	1
1 oz	Flaked almonds	25 g
2 tbsp	Milk sweetened with icing sugar	2x15 ml

Preheat the oven to 400°F (200°C) Gas 6.

Mix chopped almonds with caster sugar and vanilla essence. Moisten with egg white until evenly combined. Add flour and gather mixture together with fingertips. Divide into "nut-sized" pieces. With lightly floured hands, roll into small cigar shapes with pointed ends. Brush each one with beaten egg and sprinkle with flaked almonds. Bend into a crescent shape.

Place on a greased baking tray and brush lightly with any remaining egg. Bake for about 10–15 minutes till evenly coloured. Remove from oven and brush immediately with sweetened milk. Using a palette knife or egg slice, carefully loosen crescents and transfer to wire rack to cool.

Shortbread fingers

Overall timing 1½ hours plus cooling

Freezing Not suitable

Makes 6

12 oz	Butter	350 g
4 oz	Caster sugar	125 g
8 oz	Plain flour	225 g
8 oz	Self-raising flour	225 g
¼ teasp	Salt	1.25 ml

Preheat the oven to 275°F (140°C) Gas 1.

Cream the butter with the sugar till pale and fluffy. Sift the two flours and salt together and work into the creamed mixture to make a dough.

Turn dough on to a floured surface and press out to a thick rectangle. Make decorative notches down the long sides by pinching with the fingers. Place on a baking tray and prick all over with a fork. Mark lines for the fingers.

Bake for 1 hour. Cool, then break into fingers on the marked lines. Dredge with extra caster sugar.

Spicy sweet fritters

Overall timing 45 minutes

Freezing Not suitable

Makes 20

9 oz	Plain flour	250 g
$\frac{1}{2}$ teasp	Ground ginger	2.5 ml
$\frac{1}{2}$ teasp	Ground allspice	2.5 ml
$\frac{1}{2}$ teasp	Ground mace	2.5 ml
	Salt	
4 oz	Icing sugar	125 g
3	Egg yolks	3
1 tbsp	Orange-flower water	15 ml
$3\frac{1}{2}$ oz	Butter	100 g
	Grated rind of 1 lemon	
	Oil for deep frying	

Sift flour, spices, pinch of salt and 3 oz (75 g) icing sugar into a bowl. Mix egg yolks and flower water with 2 tbsp (2x15 ml) cold water. Add to bowl with butter and rind. Mix to a soft dough.

Roll out dough till $\frac{1}{4}$ inch (6 mm) thick. Cut out fancy shapes with pastry cutters.

Heat oil in a deep-fryer to 340°F (170°C). Fry biscuits, a few at a time, for about 5 minutes till golden. Drain on kitchen paper. Sift the remaining icing sugar over.

Golden arcs

Overall timing 30 minutes

Freezing Not suitable

Makes 30

8 oz	Fine cornmeal	225 g
6 oz	Plain flour	175 g
2 teasp	Ground cardamom	2x5 ml
$\frac{1}{2}$ teasp	Ground coriander	2.5 ml
4 oz	Caster sugar	125 g
$\frac{1}{4}$ teasp	Vanilla essence	1.25 ml
8 oz	Butter	225 g
4	Egg yolks	4

Preheat the oven to 400°F (200°C) Gas 6.

Sift the cornmeal, flour and spices into a bowl and stir in the sugar. Add the vanilla, butter and egg yolks and mix to a soft dough.

Put the mixture into a piping bag fitted with a star nozzle and pipe in 3 inch (7.5 cm) lengths on to a greased and floured baking tray. Bake for about 15 minutes till golden. Remove from the oven and allow to cool for 5 minutes. Transfer to a wire rack and leave to cool completely.

Potato surprises

Overall timing 1 hour

Freezing Suitable: fry for 2 minutes only; fry again from frozen

Makes 24

1½ lb	Floury potatoes	700 g
	Salt	
2 tbsp	Caster sugar	2x15 ml
3 fl oz	Warm milk	90 ml
½ oz	Butter	15 g
4 oz	Plain flour	125 g
	Oil for deep frying	
	Icing sugar	

Scrub potatoes, place in pan, cover with cold salted water and bring to the boil. Cook for 20–25 minutes till tender, then drain, peel and mash.

Roll out mashed potato on lightly floured surface till smooth, then place in bowl and add sugar, milk and melted butter. Stir well, gradually adding flour till soft and smooth.

Heat oil in deep-fryer to 360°F (180°C).

Roll out potato mixture and cut into rounds. Fry, a few at a time, for 4 minutes on each side. Drain on kitchen paper. Sprinkle with sifted icing sugar and serve warm.

Apple and beer puffs

Overall timing 40 minutes

Freezing Not suitable

Makes 20

2	Eggs	2
3 fl oz	Beer	90 ml
4 oz	Plain flour	125 g
	Pinch of salt	
1½ lb	Dessert apples	700 g
	Oil for frying	
	Caster sugar	
	Ground cinnamon	

Separate the eggs. Put the yolks, beer, flour and salt into a bowl and beat to a smooth batter. In another bowl, beat the egg whites till stiff, then fold into the batter. Peel, core and grate apples and mix into the batter.

Heat oil in a deep-fryer to 360°F (180°C).

Slide spoonfuls of the apple batter into the hot oil and fry for about 5 minutes or until crisp. Turn them over once during cooking. Drain on kitchen paper and roll in caster sugar, or caster sugar and cinnamon mixed together. Serve hot.

Iced marzipan biscuits

Overall timing 1½ hours plus cooling

Freezing Not suitable

Makes 30

14 oz	Plain flour	400 g
7 oz	Caster sugar	200 g
	Pinch of salt	
1	Large egg	1
7 oz	Butter	200 g
Filling and icing		
8 oz	Marzipan	225 g
5½ oz	Icing sugar	165 g
1 tbsp	Rum	15 ml
	Lemon or almond essence	
4 oz	Apricot jam	125 g
2 tbsp	Water	2x15 ml

Sift flour, sugar and salt into a bowl. Add egg and butter, cut into small pieces. Quickly knead together to form a smooth dough. Chill for 30 minutes.

Preheat the oven to 350°F (180°C) Gas 4.

Roll out dough to ¼ inch (6 mm) thickness. Cut out small shapes with a pastry cutter and place on a greased baking tray. Bake for 15 minutes.

Meanwhile, knead marzipan, 2 oz (50 g) icing sugar, rum and a few drops of essence together. Roll out to ⅛ inch (3 mm) thickness on a board dusted with icing sugar. Cut out shapes using the same cutter as for the pastry.

Remove pastry shapes from oven and immediately spread thickly with jam. Sandwich a piece of marzipan between two hot biscuits. Work quickly – the hot biscuits and jam need to adhere to the marzipan. Lift off baking trays and place on wire rack.

To make icing, mix together remaining icing sugar, a little almond essence and water and use to coat the warm biscuits. Leave to dry and cool.

Lemon refrigerator cookies

Overall timing 20 minutes plus overnight chilling

Freezing Suitable: bake after thawing

Makes 48

8 oz	Plain flour	225 g
1 teasp	Baking powder	5 ml
4 oz	Butter	125 g
3 oz	Caster sugar	75 g
	Grated rind of 2 lemons	
½ teasp	Ground cinnamon	2.5 ml
1	Egg	1

Sift flour and baking powder into a bowl. Rub in butter till mixture resembles fine breadcrumbs. Add sugar, lemon rind and cinnamon, then beat the egg and mix well into the dough.

Shape the mixture into one or two sausage shapes about 1½ inches (4 cm) in diameter. Wrap in foil, twisting the ends to seal. Chill overnight.

Preheat the oven to 375°F (190°C) Gas 5.

Remove dough from foil wrapper and thinly slice. Place slices on greased baking trays. Bake for 10–12 minutes, till golden. Cool on wire rack.

Macaroons

Overall timing 2½ hours

Freezing Not suitable

Makes 55

4	Egg whites	4
12 oz	Caster sugar	350 g
11 oz	Ground almonds	300 g
	Grated rind of 1 orange	
	Grated rind of 1 lemon	
	Pinch of salt	
1 teasp	Ground cinnamon	5 ml
½ teasp	Ground cardamom	2.5 ml

Preheat the oven to 275°F (140°C) Gas 1.

Whisk the egg whites till stiff. Gradually whisk in the caster sugar, a spoonful at a time. Fold in the almonds, orange and lemon rind, salt and spices.

Place heaped teaspoonfuls of mixture on baking trays lined with rice paper. Put on the middle and lower shelves of the oven and leave to dry for 1½–2 hours. Halfway through, swap trays round.

Cool on baking trays. Break paper from around each macaroon.

Rhine biscuits

Overall timing 45 minutes plus chilling

Freezing Not suitable

Makes 30

9 oz	Plain flour	250 g
1 teasp	Ground cinnamon	5 ml
½ teasp	Ground cloves	2.5 ml
6 oz	Butter	175 g
4 oz	Caster sugar	125 g
	Grated rind of 1 lemon	
1	Egg	1
5 tbsp	Milk	5x15 ml

Sift the flour and spices into a bowl. Add the butter and rub in till the mixture resembles fine breadcrumbs. Stir in the sugar and lemon rind. Add the egg and enough milk to make a stiff dough. Knead lightly and chill for 1 hour.

Preheat the oven to 350°F (180°C) Gas 4.

Roll out the dough on a floured board till ¼ inch (6 mm) thick, then cut out shapes with a pastry cutter. Arrange on a greased and floured baking tray. Bake for 15–20 minutes till golden. Remove from the oven and leave to cool for 3 minutes. Transfer to a wire rack and leave to cool completely.

Pastry horns

Overall timing 4½ hours

Freezing Suitable: shape and bake after thawing

Makes 6

9 oz	Plain flour	250 g
	Pinch of salt	
8 oz	Butter	225 g
4 fl oz	Cold water	120 ml
1	Egg	1
	Caster sugar	
	Whipped cream	
	Jam	

Sift flour and salt into a bowl. Rub in half the butter, then add water and mix to a dough. Chill for 1 hour. Chill remaining butter.

Place chilled butter between two sheets of greaseproof paper and roll out to a 5x3 inch (13x8 cm) rectangle.

Roll out dough on floured surface to 10x8 inch (25x20 cm) rectangle. Put butter in centre. Fold down top third over butter, then fold up bottom third. Turn so that folds are to the side. Roll out to 5x14 inch (13x36 cm) rectangle and fold again as before. Chill for 15 minutes.

Repeat the rolling, turning and folding four more times, chilling between each process.

Preheat the oven to 425°F (220°C) Gas 7.

Roll out dough to ⅛ inch (3 mm) thick. Trim to a 15x6 inch (38x15 cm) rectangle, then cut into six 1 inch (2.5 cm) strips. Glaze the strips with beaten egg, then wrap them, glazed side out, round six pastry horn moulds, starting at the point and overlapping the dough slightly.

Place on a baking tray and dredge with caster sugar. Bake for 10 minutes till crisp and golden. Slide off the moulds and cool.

Fill the horns with cream and jam.

Palmiers

Overall timing 1½ hours plus chilling

Freezing Suitable: shape and bake after thawing

Makes 12–16

8 oz	Plain flour	225 g
½ teasp	Salt	2.5 ml
6 oz	Butter	175 g
2 teasp	Lemon juice	2x5 ml
¼ pint	Cold water	150 ml
	Caster sugar	

Sift flour and salt into a bowl and rub in 1½ oz (40 g) butter. Mix in lemon juice and enough water to make a soft but not sticky dough. Knead till smooth.

Roll out dough on floured surface to 15x5 inch (38x13 cm) rectangle. Divide remaining butter into three and cut into small pieces. Dot one-third of butter over top two-thirds of dough. Fold up bottom third, then fold top third over it. Press edges to seal and turn dough so folds are to the side.

Repeat rolling out, adding another third of fat and folding, then chill for 15 minutes.

Repeat process again, using rest of butter, and chill for 15 minutes.

Preheat the oven to 425°F (220°C) Gas 7.

Roll out dough to ¼ inch (6 mm) thick. Sprinkle with caster sugar. Fold the long sides in to meet at the centre and sprinkle again with sugar. Fold the long sides in again to make four layers. Cut across folds to make ½ inch (12.5 mm) slices.

Arrange slices on dampened baking tray and flatten slightly. Bake for 6 minutes on each side. Serve warm.

Mille feuilles

Overall timing 40 minutes plus cooling

Freezing Not suitable

Makes 6

7½ oz	Frozen puff pastry	212 g
1 pint	Milk	560 ml
	Pinch of salt	
1	Vanilla pod	1
	Strip of lemon rind	
4 oz	Caster sugar	125 g
4	Medium eggs	4
1 oz	Plain flour	25 g
2 tbsp	Rum	2x15 ml
	Icing sugar	

Thaw pastry. Preheat the oven to 425°F (220°C) Gas 7.

Put the milk, salt, vanilla pod and lemon rind into a saucepan and bring to the boil. Remove from the heat and infuse for 10 minutes.

Beat together the sugar, eggs and flour in a bowl till smooth. Gradually strain the milk into the bowl, stirring, then pour the mixture back into the saucepan. Bring to the boil, stirring, and simmer till thick. Stir in the rum. Remove from the heat. Cover with damp greaseproof paper and cool.

Halve dough and roll out into two rectangles, 12x4 inches (30x10 cm). Trim edges and knock up. Place on dampened baking trays. Mark one rectangle into six 2 inch (5 cm) slices with a sharp, pointed knife. Bake for about 10 minutes till well risen and golden. Allow to cool.

Place unmarked pastry rectangle on a board and spread with custard. Place marked pastry rectangle on top and dredge well with icing sugar. Cut into slices along marked lines. Eat same day.

Iced strawberry tartlets

Overall timing 40 minutes

Freezing Not suitable

Makes 4

6 oz	Rich shortcrust pastry	175 g
4 oz	Gooseberry jam	125 g
2 tbsp	Sherry	2x15 ml
12 oz	Strawberries	350 g
1 pint	Vanilla ice cream or lemon sorbet	560 ml

Preheat the oven to 375°F (190°C) Gas 5. Put baking tray in oven to heat.

Divide dough into four. Put one-quarter into each of four 3 inch (7.5 cm) tartlet dishes and press into shape. Prick bottoms with a fork and place on heated baking tray. Bake for about 25 minutes till crisp and golden. Remove from the oven and leave to cool completely.

Meanwhile, put the jam and sherry into a saucepan and heat gently till melted. Sieve into a sauceboat and leave to cool.

Hull the strawberries. Cut a quarter of them in half lengthways and put the rest into a serving dish.

Arrange the tartlets on a serving dish. Put a scoop of ice cream or sorbet into each and decorate with halved strawberries. Serve immediately with remaining strawberries and gooseberry sauce.

Mince pies

Overall timing 30 minutes

Freezing Suitable: bake from frozen in 425°F (220°C) Gas 7 oven for 20–30 minutes

Makes 15–20

8 oz	Shortcrust pastry	225 g
8 oz	Mincemeat	225 g
3 tbsp	Brandy	3x15 ml
6 tbsp	Milk	6x15 ml
2 tbsp	Caster sugar	2x15 ml

Preheat the oven to 400°F (200°C) Gas 6.

Roll out the dough on a floured surface. Stamp out 20 rounds with a 2½ inch (6.5 cm) cutter, then 20 rounds with a 2 inch (5 cm) cutter. Press the larger rounds into a greased 20-hole bun tray.

Mix the mincemeat and brandy in a small bowl and divide between the pastry cases. Dip small dough rounds in the milk, then place one on each pie. Using a fork, press the edges together firmly to seal.

Sprinkle the caster sugar over the top. Bake for about 20 minutes till golden. Serve hot or cold.

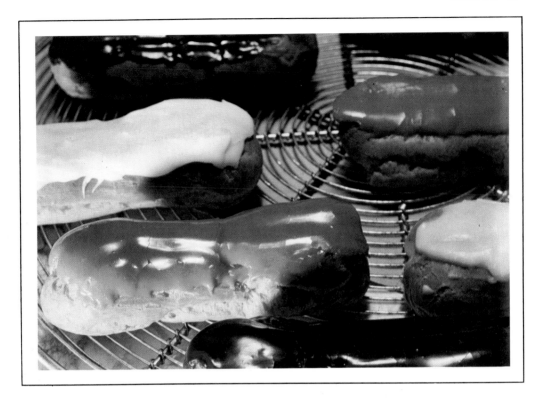

Eclairs

Overall timing 1½ hours

Freezing Suitable: bake from frozen

Makes 16

4 oz	Choux paste	125 g
½ pint	Whipping cream	300 ml
2 tbsp	Caster sugar	2x15 ml
4 oz	Icing sugar	125 g
2 teasp	Drinking chocolate	2x5 ml
1–2 tbsp	Hot water	1–2x 15 ml

Preheat the oven to 425°F (220°C) Gas 7.

Spoon paste into piping bag fitted with ½ inch (12.5 mm) plain nozzle and pipe fingers, about 3 inches (7.5 cm) long, on greased baking trays. Leave plenty of space between fingers so they have room to expand during baking. Bake for about 30 minutes till golden and crisp. Transfer to a wire rack. Make a slit down side of each éclair to allow steam to escape and leave to cool.

Whip cream with sugar until just thick and holding soft peaks. Spoon cream into cooled éclairs and return to wire rack placed over greaseproof paper.

Mix icing sugar with drinking chocolate and hot water. The glacé icing should be thick enough to coat the back of a spoon. If too thick, add a little more water; if too runny, add more icing sugar. Dip top of one éclair at a time into icing. Leave on wire rack till icing is set. Eat the same day.

Soured cream pastries

Overall timing 10 minutes plus chilling

Freezing Not suitable

Makes 20

12 oz	Plain flour	350 g
6 oz	Butter	175 g
1	Egg yolk	1
¼ pint	Carton of soured cream	150 ml
Filling		
8 oz	Cream cheese	225 g
2 oz	Caster sugar	50 g
2 oz	Sultanas	50 g

Sift flour into a bowl and rub in the butter till the mixture resembles fine breadcrumbs. Add the egg yolk and soured cream and mix with a palette knife to make a soft dough. Chill for 1 hour.

Mix together the cream cheese, sugar and sultanas.

Preheat the oven to 400°F (200°C) Gas 6.

Roll out the dough and cut out 40 rounds with a fluted 2 inch (5 cm) cutter. Put a spoonful of the filling on to half the rounds, then cover with the remaining rounds and press the edges together to seal. Arrange on a baking sheet and bake for 25 minutes till golden brown.

Jam puffs

Overall timing 20 minutes plus thawing

Freezing Not suitable

Makes 12

7½ oz	Frozen puff pastry	212 g
1	Egg	1
5 tbsp	Jam	5 x 15 ml

Thaw pastry. Preheat the oven to 425°F (220°C) Gas 7.

Roll out dough to ¼ inch (6 mm) thickness. Cut into 2 inch (5 cm) rounds with a pastry cutter. Mark the centres with a small cutter or a bottle lid. Do not cut through.

Place on a dampened baking tray and brush with beaten egg. Bake for about 10 minutes till well risen and golden. Cool on a wire rack.

Remove centres and put a heaped teaspoon of jam in each. Use centres of pastry as lids, if liked. Serve warm.

Irish apple turnovers

Overall timing 2 hours including refrigeration

Freezing Suitable: refresh in 350°F (180°C) Gas 4 oven for 10–15 minutes

Makes 20 small or 12 large

9 oz	Plain flour	250 g
2 teasp	Baking powder	2x5 ml
5 oz	Caster sugar	150 g
5 oz	Butter	150 g
2 tbsp	Cold water	2x15 ml
1 lb	Cox's Orange Pippins	450 g
1 tbsp	Apricot jam	15 ml
2 tbsp	Mixed dried fruit	2x15 ml
	Icing sugar	

Sift flour, baking powder and sugar into a bowl and make a well in the centre. Cut the softened butter into small pieces and put round the edge. Add water and knead to make a smooth dough. Chill for 1 hour.

Preheat the oven to 350°F (180°C) Gas 4.

Core apples. Place them on a baking tray and bake for 20 minutes till tender. Peel them, then mash and mix with the apricot jam and dried fruit.

Increase the oven temperature to 400°F (200°C) Gas 6.

Roll out dough on a lightly floured board to ⅛ inch (3 mm) thickness. Cut out rounds or squares. Spoon a little apple mixture into the centre of each dough shape. Moisten edges with water, fold the dough over to form a half moon, triangle or rectangle, and press edges well together. Place on a greased baking tray.

Bake for 15–20 minutes. Dredge with icing sugar and serve warm with whipped cream or vanilla ice cream.

Choux buns

Overall timing 1½ hours plus cooling

Freezing Not suitable

Makes 8

4 oz	Choux paste	125 g
¾ pint	Creamy milk	400 ml
	Vanilla pod	
	Grated rind of 1 lemon and 1 orange	
4	Eggs	4
8 tbsp	Caster sugar	8x15 ml
4 tbsp	Plain flour	4x15 ml
	Salt	
2 tbsp	Icing sugar	2x15 ml

Preheat the oven to 425°F (220°C) Gas 7.

Place choux paste in eight spoonfuls on a greased baking tray, shaping into mounds about 2 inches (5 cm) in diameter, and leaving space between them to allow for rising. Bake for 20 minutes till doubled in size.

Reduce the temperature to 375°F (190°C) Gas 5 and bake for a further 10–15 minutes till crusty and golden. Switch off the oven. Cut a slit in each puff to release steam, then return to oven, leaving door open, to dry and cool.

Meanwhile, make filling. Put milk, vanilla pod and grated rinds into a saucepan and heat till almost boiling. Remove from heat, cover and infuse for 10 minutes.

Separate eggs. Beat yolks with 6 tbsp (6x15 ml) caster sugar and the flour. Remove vanilla pod from milk and gradually add to the egg yolks, whisking constantly. Return to pan and bring to the boil, stirring. Simmer till thick. Remove from heat.

Whisk egg whites with a pinch of salt till stiff. Whisk in remaining caster sugar, then fold into warm custard. Cool, then chill.

Fill choux puffs with custard and dredge with icing sugar.

Almond tartlets

Overall timing 1 hour plus cooling

Freezing Suitable: ice and decorate after thawing

Makes 12

14 oz	Shortcrust pastry	400 g
4	Eggs	4
3½ oz	Caster sugar	100 g
4 oz	Ground almonds	125 g
Decoration		
5 oz	Icing sugar	150 g
1 tbsp	Milk	15 ml
1 tbsp	Lemon juice	15 ml
12	Glacé cherries	12
	Angelica leaves	

Preheat the oven to 400°F (200°C) Gas 6.

Roll out the dough and use to line 12 tartlet tins. Bake blind for 10 minutes, then remove from oven.

Separate the eggs. Add sugar to yolks and whisk together till pale and thick. Fold in ground almonds. In another bowl, whisk egg whites till stiff, then fold into almond mixture.

Fill pastry cases with almond mixture. Place on a baking tray and bake for 15–20 minutes till centre is firm and springy. Leave to cool.

Sift the icing sugar into a bowl and beat in milk and lemon juice till smooth. Spread over tartlets. Decorate with whole glacé cherries and angelica leaves and leave till set.

Blackcurrant boats

Overall timing 1 hour 20 minutes

Freezing Not suitable

Makes 8

3 oz	Plain flour	75 g
1½ oz	Caster sugar	40 g
1	Egg	1
	Vanilla essence	
1½ oz	Butter	40 g
Filling		
11 oz	Can of blackcurrants	300 g
2 oz	Caster sugar	50 g
1 oz	Flaked almonds	25 g
¼ pint	Carton of double cream	150 ml
1 tbsp	Icing sugar	15 ml

Preheat the oven to 425°F (220°C) Gas 7.

Sift flour into a bowl, make a well in the centre and add sugar, egg and a few drops of vanilla essence. Add the butter, cut into pieces, and knead to a dough. Chill for 30 minutes.

Roll out dough to ¼ inch (6 mm) thick and use to line eight barquette tins. Prick and bake blind for 15–20 minutes till cooked and golden brown. Cool.

Drain blackcurrants and place in bowl. Sprinkle over the caster sugar and leave for 1 hour.

Preheat the grill. Spread flaked almonds on grill pan and toast. Whip cream till stiff with icing sugar. Spoon into piping bag.

Drain blackcurrants and divide between pastry boats. Pipe on cream and decorate with toasted almonds.

Baklava

Overall timing 1½ hours

Freezing Suitable

Makes 8

4 oz	Unsalted butter	125 g
1 lb	Ready-made phyllo pastry	450 g
8 oz	Walnuts, almonds or pistachios	225 g
2 tbsp	Caster sugar	2x15 ml
½ teasp	Ground cinnamon	2.5 ml
Syrup		
4 oz	Clear honey	125 g
¼ pint	Water	150 ml
2 tbsp	Lemon juice	2x15 ml

Preheat the oven to 425°F (220°C) Gas 7.

Melt the butter in a small saucepan and brush a little over the bottom and sides of a 10x8 inch (25x20 cm) roasting tin.

Layer half the pastry sheets in the tin, brushing liberally with butter between each sheet, and folding in the edges so that sheets fit the tin. Keep rest of the pastry covered to prevent it drying out.

Mix together the chopped nuts, sugar and cinnamon and spread over pastry. Cover with remaining pastry layers, brushing each with butter. Brush the top layer well with any remaining butter.

Cut through the top two layers of pastry with a sharp knife to divide into four widthways, then cut each quarter in half diagonally so you have eight triangles. Bake for 15 minutes, then reduce heat to 350°F (180°C) Gas 4 and bake for a further 25–30 minutes till well risen and golden.

Meanwhile, make the syrup. Melt the honey in the water and add the lemon juice. Allow to cool.

Remove baklava from oven, pour cold syrup over and leave to cool in tin. Cut along the marked lines to serve.

Rum and almond pastry cake

Overall timing $2\frac{1}{4}$ hours

Freezing Suitable: refresh from frozen in 350°F (180°C) Gas 4 oven for 30 minutes

Serves 6–8

13 oz	Frozen puff pastry	375 g
3 oz	Butter	75 g
3 oz	Caster sugar	75 g
2	Eggs	2
4 oz	Ground almonds	125 g
2 tbsp	Rum	2x15 ml
1 tbsp	Icing sugar	15 ml

Thaw pastry. To make filling, cream butter with sugar till light and fluffy. Beat in one whole egg and one egg yolk, reserving white. Fold in the ground almonds and rum. Cover and chill for 40 minutes.

Roll out dough to $\frac{1}{4}$ inch (6 mm) thickness. Cut out two rounds, one 8 inch (20 cm) and the other 9 inch (23 cm). Place smaller one on a dampened baking tray. Place almond filling in a ball in centre of dough round, leaving at least a 2 inch (5 cm) border all round. Brush edges with water.

Place second dough round on top and press edges together to seal. Using a knife, trim, then knock up edges and crimp. Chill for 15 minutes.

Preheat the oven to 450°F (230°C) Gas 8.

Brush pie with reserved beaten egg white. Leave for 1 minute, then brush again. Using the tip of a sharp knife, score top of pie to make a swirl pattern. Bake for 20 minutes, then reduce temperature to 400°F (200°C) Gas 6 and bake for a further 25 minutes, or until well risen and golden brown.

Remove from oven and increase heat to 475°F (240°C) Gas 9. Sift icing sugar over pie and return to oven to bake for 4–5 minutes to glaze. Remove from baking tray with palette knife and place on serving plate.

Index